RELUCTANT RETURN

JEWISH LITERATURE AND CULTURE

Series Editor, Alvin H. Rosenfeld

RELUCTANT RETURN

A SURVIVOR'S JOURNEY TO
AN AUSTRIAN TOWN

DAVID W. WEISS

INDIANA
UNIVERSITY
PRESS

Bloomington & Indianapolis

This book is a publication of

Indiana University Press
601 North Morton Street
Bloomington, Indiana 47404-3797 USA

www.indiana.edu/~iupress

Telephone orders   800-842-6796
Fax orders   812-855-7931
Orders by e-mail   iuporder@indiana.edu

© 1999 by David W. Weiss

The paper used in this publication meets the minimum
requirements of American National Standard for Information
Sciences—Permanence of Paper for Printed Library
Materials, ANSI Z39.48-1984.

Manufactured in the United States of America

Library of Congress Cataloging-in-Publication Data

Weiss, David W., date
Reluctant return : a survivor's journey to an Austrian town / David W. Weiss.
p.   cm. — (Jewish literature and culture)
ISBN 0-253-33584-1 (cl : alk. paper)
1. Weiss, David W., date. 2. Jews—Austria—Wiener Neustadt—Biography.
3. Holocaust, Jewish (1939–1945)—Austria—Wiener Neustadt—Personal narratives.
4. Jews, Austrian—Israel—Travel—Austria—Wiener Neustadt. 5. Wiener Neustadt (Austria)—Ethnic relations.   I. Title.   II. Series.
DS135.A93W226   1999
943.6'12—dc21   99-11005
[B]

1   2   3   4   5   04   03   02   01   00   99

*This book is published
with the generous sponsorship of*

J. WILLIAM AND FRANCES B. JULIAN

CONTENTS

ACKNOWLEDGMENTS

The idea for this book was seeded by Hillel Daleski, Professor of English Literature at Hebrew University, and Shirley Kaufman, the poet. Good friends, they listened to me spill out my story of confused excitement one evening over drinks in Jerusalem shortly after I came home from the *Woche der Begegnung* in Wiener Neustadt, the town in which I grew up. They urged me to record the story of what brought that week about and what I was trying to make of it, and they introduced me to the writer Eric Silver. In November of 1995, the *Jerusalem Report* published a brief account by Mr. Silver under the title "A Reluctant Return."

All right, I thought, that's done, the tale told, and now back to work on a couple of research papers in psychoneuroimmunology, an area of research in which I had recently taken an interest. But I could not shake off the impressions and ambivalence engendered by the return to the country of my youth. I found myself endlessly talking about the week. Laurie Blitzer, a young woman related to my wife's family, was staying with us in Jerusalem and bore the brunt of the flow. She thought I should write the story myself, expanding on the *Report*'s article. Laurie is a persuasive woman, and during a sabbatical in New York a year later I started scribbling. I intended no more than a few dozen pages at the most, but I have often been regarded an ink-spot by professional colleagues, and the pages took on a life of their own, reproducing as if by an autochthonous process, a binary fission of print. Somewhere along the way I showed a few sections to new acquaintances. Joelle Sander, Professor of English at Sarah Lawrence College; the psychiatrist Fred Sander who had also ventured a brief return to his native Germany; Leo Goldberger, Professor of Psychology at New York University; and Dr. Carol Rittner, R.S.M., believed I should continue. This is the result.

Hillel Daleski went over and improved a draft with the painstaking care he would give a doctoral dissertation, and introduced me to Alvin H. Rosenfeld, Professor of English and Director of the Jewish Studies Program at Indiana University. Dr. Rosenfeld read the manuscript and recommended it to Dr. Janet Rabinowitch, Senior Editor at Indiana University Press. Modesty is surely not a virtue of mine, but I am still astounded at the generous acceptance that followed.

I am deeply grateful to them all for advice and encouragement, far greater than I had any reason to expect; and to Dana Groehl, who struggled with hundreds of handwritten and badly typed sheets and made them digestible for the computer, an instrument whose perplexing mysteries I have so far left undisturbed.

And for Judy, my wife, who with a falcon's eye considered and then ripped apart page after faulty page of my proudest efforts, transmuting them into a manuscript: Gratitude is a small word, too small to tell of her help and her sufferance of my frequent outbursts of enraged vanity. I acknowledge her contribution with love and admiration.

DAVID W. WEISS
JERUSALEM
JULY 1998

RELUCTANT RETURN

Chapter 1

A CALL FROM HELMUTH EIWEN

DECEMBER 1993, JERUSALEM

My secretary announces a call from Zurich: "The man sounds Israeli. He says you don't know each other."

We don't. He represents an Israeli organization in Switzerland and Austria, and he has been asked by an acquaintance from Wiener Neustadt (Wr. Neustadt), in Niederösterreich, for help in tracing a person who as a child had lived in that town under the name of Weiss. The object of the search was the son of the rabbi who had served Wr. Neustadt and the neighboring towns and villages until after the Anschluss in 1938. There was reason to believe that the family had found refuge in America, and that the son was working as a scientist at a university in Israel. The search might prove to be a difficult one. Many immigrants to Israel Hebraicize their names, and there was very little else to go on. Chaim Kol, the caller, had offered to try. He had scanned the catalogues of the country's institutions of higher learning and then the telephone directories of those cities. He had already contacted several Dr. Weisses; I was next on his list.

Yes, he has located the right one. I am professor of immunology at the Hebrew University in Jerusalem, and my father, who died in 1954 in New York, a decade before I made the move to Israel, had been Oberrabbiner of those Austrian communities.

Who wanted to reach me, and why?, I ask Kol.

"His name is Helmuth Eiwen. He is pastor of a small, independent

Protestant congregation, a *Freikirche,* which he and his wife founded some years ago. Pentecostals, I think. They are called the *Ichthys Gemeinde.* They have been active in Jewish and Israeli causes. The Eiwens are in Jerusalem right now, at an assembly of European *Freikirchen.* They and their people come frequently to demonstrate support and to volunteer. Are you willing to talk with him? He is reluctant to call you directly . . . perhaps you don't want to have anything to do with Christian clergy from that place?"

I hesitate for more than a few seconds. The pastor's reticence is not unfounded. I have wanted nothing to do with things Austrian since we made our escape. The memories are bitter. Memories of a damaged youth. I am a survivor. What I survived is an old, hard hatred that burst through its thin restraints. As long as the hatred was kept in check, muted, that was normalcy, par for the course for Austria's Jews. When it was released, it became the Holocaust.

Holocaust survivor . . . that usually connotes the few who lived through the death camps. My family and I were more fortunate. We got out, by a slim margin, before the transports started for the East; someone took a risk; we were helped. Still . . . a surviving is involved. Survival of the human self. The people among whom I grew up declared one day in 1938 that Jews were not really of the human species; to have thought that they were had been a grave mistake. In the light of that discovery, I stood bare, no longer *Mensch,* debased in all my aspects down to my blood and genes. Perhaps the threat to identity is especially damaging in the years a boy passes to manhood: If I am a nonperson, what then am I, how can I move on?

The bitterness has been sustained. Since the end of the war, Austria has not found it in its national soul to make even the gestures of acknowledgment and regret that Germany has. Austria has consistently claimed to have been a victim of Nazi aggression. In truth, Austrians contributed a disproportionate share to the cause of Jewish extermination. The image of the Gemütlichkeit that so smoothly turned to murderousness is repellent.

And yet, I think in these seconds, the pastor has displayed a sensitivity in his reticence. And they come to Israel to be of help. I have always held to the belief that when one stands face to face with another human being the encounter must be with the individual, *tabula rasa,* no matter how strong and how justified the animosity toward the collective. I have, in fact, been back to Austria, under very special circumstances, and I have met with exceptional people from the land that so long ago had been home. Just perhaps, this might be another such exceptional meeting.

I ask Kol to give the pastor my telephone number. Less than half an hour later Helmuth Eiwen rings. The brief conversation is long enough to persuade me to meet him. I ask the Eiwens to join us for Sabbath eve dinner that Friday night in our home. The meal together turns out to be the beginning of a remarkable and confusing episode in my life.

Kiddush is read, and after the ceremonial washing of hands the blessing over bread is recited. The *challoth* are uncovered on the oval porcelain platter embellished with a design of flowers and the legend "In Honor of the Sabbath," a gift from Christian Arab friends from Nazareth. The plate is set on our table every Friday night; the Sabbath is meant to be a moment of peace, an instant wrested from quotidian time. The bread is broken and sprinkled with salt, as once the high priest of the temple dusted salt on the sacrifice brought to the altar. Salt stands for permanence. I explain the meanings, layer upon layer, of the Sabbath meal's symbols. The Eiwens know little of Jewish religious custom. They do know something, however, of the history of the Jews, and especially of those periods in which Jewish and Christian experience have intersected. During the meal and for hours thereafter, they relate the story of what finally brought them to us in the quest for the son of the rabbi of Wr. Neustadt.

Chapter 2

ICHTHYS: A MISSION

I take Helmuth to be about fifty, his wife Uli a few years younger. There is nothing striking in their appearance. He has light brown hair, already sparse, and is of average height and build. She is shorter and heavy, blonde, and with her large round face and fair complexion could have stepped out of a picture postcard of Austrian peasant women on a Sunday afternoon stroll. But when they speak, they are transformed. They seem nearly incapable of small talk, both on that night and all the many times we have been together since; they speak of what impels their lives. Then they light up with a startling intensity. Their expressions, the eyes and the gestures of hands and body, convey the importuning of a force that will not be contained.

The Eiwens are overwhelmingly absorbed in a mission. That is to regain for themselves, for their community and town, and for all Christianity the favor of God. They are deeply, wholly committed Christians. They accept Jesus of Nazareth as the Messiah and his passion on the cross as redemptive, but they address God as the God of Abraham, Isaac, and Jacob; and his vow to the Patriarch, "And I will bless them that bless thee, and him that curseth thee will I curse; and in thee shall all the families of the earth be blessed," has for them an exhortative immediacy. In their persecutions of the Jews, Christians have forced God to turn his face away. His countenance will not again illuminate the Christian world until amends are made to his chosen people.

The Eiwens have pledged themselves to a specific task, to restore God to Wr. Neustadt. He was banished, they believe, together with the Jews in the edict of expulsion issued by the Emperor Maximilian I in

1496. The edict intended to expel them forever. It was nearly three centuries before they could begin drifting back. Wr. Neustadt had early acquired a reputation for a prurient Jew hatred. There is a large medieval stone tablet on display in the local museum depicting a sow from whose teats a group of rabbis—so the engraved legend reads—ravenously suckle; it was called the *Judenspott*, the mocking of the Jews, and had once been displayed in the market place. Even in my youth, the ambience of daily anti-Semitism was palpable. Immediately after the Anschluss, the exclusion of the Jews from society and their treatment by the populace had an edge of barbarity that set the tone for the more lethal persecutions that soon followed. In the last weeks of the war, thousands of Jews who had survived death marches from neighboring Hungary succumbed to savage mistreatment in the snows at Wöllersdorf and other suburbs. Not a Jew remains today in the town and its environs. The Eiwens ascribe the "empty, godless secularism" of the region to the withdrawal of God's presence, and they are dedicated to lifting the curse.

But that cannot be accomplished by Christians alone. The channel to grace regained can only be the Jews, and if the Eiwens are to dwell in a city of God, it is the aging, scattered survivors of Wr. Neustadt's once flourishing Jewish community who must be the agents.

It is late. The electricity has been turned off by the automated Sabbath clock. We sit in the flickering light of the candles and the Eiwens make their plea. Would I return to Wr. Neustadt for a week of meetings with their community, and with whatever other groups—schoolchildren, unions, the municipality—they could persuade to join in the occasion, *"Eine Woche der Begegnung"*? Would I place them in contact with other former Wr. Neustädters in Israel and abroad and help enlist their participation? I am, they point out, the only son of the town's last Jewish spiritual leader and perhaps something of the mantle of leadership has devolved on me that would endorse my advocacy.

They make it clear that they can invite us only in the name of their own congregation. The official recognized churches in Austria are Roman Catholic and Lutheran. A *Freikirche* such as theirs is considered a sect. They are isolated from the civic life of the town, are regarded with, at best, aloofness, and often with animosity. That the members of their small community, about 140 families, have left the established denominations for a more intimate, vibrant Christianity has not endeared them to the townspeople, whose personal religious involvements, if any, may indeed tend toward rote and nonchalance, but who scorn deviant alternatives. The idea of a *Begegnung* with Wr. Neustadt's dispersed Jews was entirely that of the Eiwens, the hospitality to be offered entirely that of the *Freikirche.*

I am quite convinced that I want nothing to do with such a "homecoming," but I am intrigued. They intend to search out every one of us who fled and is still living, to reconstitute for one week the rapidly dwindling remnants of the *kehillah* on its old home ground. I point out that I know of at least thirty Wr. Neustadt Jews in Israel and of a few more in America, South America, Great Britain; there may be still others in other reaches of our Diaspora. Have the Eiwens really considered the cost of travel and accommodation if even only some of us would accept? That is not at all a question, they reply. True, they are not an affluent community, most of them are artisans and white-collar employees, but each family contributes a tithe of its monthly income to the *Gemeinde,* and what they lack God will show them how to make up. There is no question. Their faith is absolute. It is God who planted the seed of this undertaking in their hearts, it is God's will and God's work, and they themselves are merely deputized to carry it out. It will not be the first time that a helping hand has miraculously reached out to them. There was an unforeseen bequest from a member's distant relative. A hoard of gold coins was discovered when floorboards of a friend's bomb-damaged building were removed for repairs. There have been anonymous gifts. That is how they built their meetinghouse and how they have managed to fund their programs for Jews and Israel.

That program has been extensive, I learn. The whole community, men, women and children, travel periodically to Israel to bear living witness to their allegiance to the nascent Jewish nation. They have walked, kilometer upon kilometer, torches in hand, the routes of the death marches from the East into the Burgenland and Niederösterreich. When they learned that many of the recent Jewish refugees from the Soviet Union who temporarily sheltered in Austrian transit camps had little knowledge of Judaism, they took them Hebrew bibles and prayer books. They did not go as missionaries of Christ. That would have been an affront to God's covenant with Abraham and his descendants. They went, rather, as envoys of the God of Abraham, Isaac, and Jacob to encourage his children to be Jews. The *Woche der Begegnung* is only their latest endeavor.

I am bewildered. I thought I had acquired a fairly broad understanding of the varieties of Christian religious experience and of Christian perceptions of the place of the Jews in the cosmos. I had known many Christian clergymen during a stint as acting Jewish chaplain in the U.S. Army at a replacement center for the European theater of operations in the late 1940s. The friendships formed then with some of the men engendered an enduring interest in the theology and history of Christian faiths. I pride myself on having once known the Latin mass by heart, and on my navigational skills through the shoals of Protestant denominational divergences. In more recent years, I have been asked to lecture at conferences sponsored by the Vatican and by the World Council of Churches on the intersections of nature, science, and religious belief. But none of the insights I have gained are of much help in unraveling the mystery to which I am introduced this Sabbath eve, and which I have found ever more perplexing as I have come to know the Eiwens and Ichthys. What kind of Christians are these, with their obsessive preoccupation with the Jewish people?

Chapter 3

ULI'S VISIONS

I chthys, the sign of the fish, is an acronym in the Greek: *Jesus Christos Theu Huyos Soter,* Jesus Christ the Son of God Is Savior. Yet in the drama of human salvation, the Jews are perceived by the people of Ichthys as elemental, constant protagonists. They are not dormant seeds who await the Christian illumination that shall one day make them and then all humankind resplendent with the eternal grace of Christ's second coming. They are, rather, as Jews, agents of redemption for all time. To Ichthys, Judaism is not a force that has spent itself in giving rise to a new and different covenant; it has not fallen by the wayside, an anachronism that might perhaps deserve a measure of historical interest and even appreciation. On the contrary. Judaism persists, uninterruptedly and dynamically, and Christian faith lies in an unbroken continuum with it. It is in the deeply resonant quality of their identification with this continuum that Ichthys has stepped beyond the trends in post–Vatican II Christianity that have begun to legitimize the perpetuity of God's covenant with Israel. For these gentile believers in the gospel of the Son of God, God the Father forever remains, not metaphorically, but with a vibrant literalness, the God of the Jewish people who have chosen Him and whom He has chosen. The Church of Christ is triumphant in Ichthys, but they behold no blindfold on the countenance of the Synagogue. Ichthys is radiant with the tensions of their self-definition.

How did they arrive at this station of their cross?

As a young, unmarried woman, Uli lived in Israel for several years in a Christian commune in the north. She developed an affection for the country and planned to stay on. But on a visit home she met Helmuth, a Lutheran priest in Neunkirchen. They fell in love, married, and began raising a family in the vicinity of his parish. Helmuth held no particular sentiments for Jews or Israel, and, as Uli puts it, regarded her Zionism as a charming peculiarity.

But Uli is a dreamer of powerful dreams, and she is a powerful personality.

She relates the first of many dreams that changed their lives, and that would have an impact on mine:

"It was past midnight, I was sleeping soundly, and suddenly there was this great bright light filling the room. Just a panel of brilliant light. Then a line formed in the middle. It seemed like an arrow, a pointer, to direct me to go somewhere. Somehow, I understood the direction. I was to go to a place at the city wall. Then the light was gone and I woke up. I felt disturbed and couldn't sleep again. The instruction was very clear, and early in the morning I went there. It was a spot to which I had not been before."

Uli found herself at a site in the medieval walls that encircle much of the town. Six ancient tombstones are immured there in a row, side by side. I had been there several times with my father, and with other Jewish children. It was a little-known place that was heavily overgrown with bushes. The Hebrew legends engraved in the stones, which date from the thirteenth century, are in large part still legible. A husband mourning his wife of valor who was taken too young, parents lamenting a child. Someone long ago had taken these remnants of the Jewish cemetery that was destroyed after an expulsion of the Jews and inserted them into the wall, not for structural support as did the Crusaders with Roman columns when they erected their fortresses in the Holy Land, but rather, it seems, as historical mementos. For us children, they were a scary reminder of bad times and transience, but they were also a source of covert pride. Look how long we've been here! Nothing else demonstrably Jewish, with the unavoidable exception of the large, Moorish-style synagogue, *der Tempel,* was visible in Wr. Neustadt even in good times. We were Austrian citizens, of course, cultured Western Jews and proud of that, with all the official rights of upstanding *Bürger,* but, nonetheless, "one need not throw one's distinctiveness into gentile faces." Enough was enough. *Man darf nicht übertreiben*—one must not overdo it. The occasional Jewish beggar with beard, earlocks, and kaftan who wandered through Austrian towns seeking alms from Jewish communities for his family in Galicia was a sufficient reminder of the ineradicable collective alienness that lay beneath our civilized garb and distinguished status.

By the time Uli found herself staring at the exotic stone markers, the brush had been cleared, a narrow slanted shingle roof had been placed above them as protection from rain and further erosion, and a small plaque identified the site as a historical landmark.

For Uli, there was also a writing on the wall, visible only to her inner eye. A command addressed to her. "I knew at once this was a call from God, that I had to find out about the Jews who live here," Uli recalls. She did not yet know that no Jew was left in the town, in the entire region. It took some effort to find out, and only then did she understand that the call had more than a merely educational intent: "I knew now that God had placed a responsibility on me."

That was the germ of an idea. If believing Christians had caused the Jews to disappear, then believing Christians had to make atonement. As she thought about Jews, passages from the Old Testament flashed in Uli's mind. She knew that the missive to her came from the God of the Patriarchs, and because it was she, a devout Christian, who had been awakened from sleep, that God was hers, too.

Helmuth, only marginally curious, was little moved. He knew that his wife had within herself a finely attuned receiver to messages from above, but he was far from certain that her ability to decode them was always precise.

But then Uli had another, more startling vision:

"Helmuth was officiating at Sunday communion service. I knelt before the altar. My head was bowed. And there suddenly stood out from the mosaic on the floor the form of a swastika."

Uli screamed and ran out. She insisted that Helmuth track down the meaning of that phantom apparition. What Helmuth discovered shook his tolerant complacency. On a Sunday shortly after the Anschluss, the Lutheran priest officiating at the altar had paused at the outset of the rite and, stripping off his priestly vestments, had stood before the congregation resplendent in S.S. uniform. "Heil Hitler!" he had shouted. *Dominus vobiscum.*

It did not take Helmuth long to learn that anti-Semitism in the Lutheran Church in Austria had been prevalent, that it was by no means exceptional for a priest to extend his devotions to the Nazi cause. Neither had the churches in the regions shown much inclination in the postwar years to acknowledge any guilt by association or by indifference. It was perhaps not only this revelation that catapulted Helmuth into a crisis of identity. He is a man of strong convictions, and he, like Uli, is alert to a summons of the spirit. He is ever the individualist. As I came to know him better, I suspected that there had long been in him a latent impatience with religious formalism and a leaning toward the charismatic. At that moment of knowing, he asked himself, as he now tells me: "Could I still remain priest in that Church, could I in the shadow of this taint continue to mediate God's sacraments?" No, he could not. The moment was for him a crossroads, a point of no return. He tendered his resignation.

He was urged to reconsider. He had a family to support and no other prospect of a livelihood. Sharp poverty would go hand in hand with the social ostracism of his desertion. But that had ceased to matter to Helmuth. What did matter was the shaking realization that he had been summoned by Abraham's God.

Helmuth underwent a metamorphosis. His thoughts and his actions would from here on be intimately informed by God. He was pledged to a task. That, he was convinced, was to fashion a clean new vessel for his Christian faith and ministry. How, he did not know. But charged with his conviction, exhilarated, Helmuth drew to himself a widening circle of others who had failed to find inspiration in the impersonal formulas and ceremonies of the conventional churches. Ichthys was born.

Chapter 4

RETURN? *NUNC MAS*

The invitation from the Eiwens was not my first to return to Austria. That had arrived by letter on my desk in Jerusalem the year that marked the passage of half a century after the *Anschluss*.

The Austrian Society for Immunology and Allergology had ventured to take notice of that milestone by inviting to its annual conference ten scientists in the field who, as carriers of more Jewish genes than was compatible with existence in Nazi Austria, had been obliged as children to flee the country. I was one of the ten.

The invitation was tactful. The society's president recognized that certain memories, certain sensibilities, might cause some of us to be reluctant. He could well understand that. But, he pointed out, there was a new Austria, things had changed, the time had come for reconciliation, for new beginnings. It was a very generous invitation. We would be the society's guests, all expenses paid. The occasion would be a festive one. We were to be honored for our scientific accomplishments and, unsaid but self-evident, for surviving. There would be receptions, greetings by dignitaries, a trip to the *Wiener Wald*.

I declined. There followed an exchange of correspondence. I learned that of the two top officers of the society, one was in fact Jewish, the other the son of a gentile family that had been opposed to National Socialism and had suffered for its opposition. I replied that my refusal was not personal, that I had only respect for the small number of Austrians who had been principled and courageous enough to dissent, that my stand was vis-à-vis the Austrian collective. I could not assent to participate in events sponsored by a representative body. The scientific associations of Austria had not lifted a finger to protect their non-Aryan members from segregation, deportation, and death. If they or any other official organization wanted seriously to embark on the long road back, that was to be applauded. But the burden of reconciliation should not be placed on the shoulders of the victim. It is not for the Jewish people to respond with facile alacrity to easy overtures. Fifty years is too soon for that. Jewish blood has soaked Austrian soil. Are we already to be deaf to its cry? We must not be, that would be a breaking of the bonds that hold us Jews together in time.

And yet I was painfully aware of the ambivalence that often undercuts my resolution when conscience and inclination conflict. I knew my weakness when a gesture of friendship is made by an enemy: I would respond with open arms. I knew that in the glow of Viennese festive graciousness I could slip quickly into comfort, into forgetfulness. I would be glad to be made to feel at home again in the place that once had been home. I have a longing for the normalcy of everyday relationships.

That clash of principle and instinct marked the two professional journeys I made to Germany earlier in my career. The first, in 1959, had been, until the last moment, unintentional. An English colleague had organized an international workshop on nonspecific immunity, a newly developing field in which I was active and had published, and I was one of a small, elite group of scientists who were asked to participate. Still very much a beginner in research, the novice among them, I was flattered. The meeting was scheduled for a town in Switzerland. Then, with only a few weeks to go, a letter arrived from Otto Westphal, the distinguished director of the Max Planck Institute in Freiburg-in-Breisgau in the German Schwarzwald just across the Swiss border, informing us of a change of venue. There were logistic complications, and the conference would now be held in the German city.

My reply to Westphal was abrupt and rude. Most assuredly, I would not come; I had rejected all contacts with Germany and Germans, and I was not about to compromise a resolve to guard my distance from evil for the rest of my days. I expected no further word. My note had left no opening, and apprentices in science do not throw gloves in the face of its masters.

To my astonishment, Westphal wrote back and then called. He was insistent that I reconsider, for precisely the reasons that caused me to excoriate any association with Germany. There was a tone of entreaty to his words. He had to show me, directly, palpably, that there were exceptions to what I believed to be the rule, that there were Germans who did not shrug off answerability, for whom it was a matter of honor to strive to repair, if only in a minuscule way, what they knew could never be made whole. What he told me then, and amplified in many later conversations, led to a lasting friendship between us.

The son of one of the few leading physicists in prewar Germany who were not Jewish, Westphal had grown up in a circle of largely Jewish acquaintances. Some of his friends had urged him to join the Nazi Party early: With a sufficient number of decent persons in its ranks, the party could be changed from within. Westphal became a member, first of the Party, and then of the S.S. When, by 1938, it was clear to him that Nazism was not about to reverse its code of anti-Semitism, violence, and jingoism, he wanted to resign. He was told that resignation would bring him before a Gestapo tribunal and a likely sentence to a concentration camp. He withdrew his resignation and remained a member of the S.S., serving during the war as head of a chemical research institute in Germany. There he protected several "racially" Jewish coworkers as vital to the laboratory's research program. He knew what transpired in the death and slave labor camps that dotted the map of Europe. He offered me no explanations, no extenuating circumstances. Since the end of the war, he had taken a leading role in German-Israeli friendship groups, had been a key supporter of science in Israel, and been involved in the expediting of funds and emergency equipment to the country during its confrontations with Arab forces. His sense of collective German guilt had been a central theme in his life. One night after many drinks in a Dixieland bar in San Francisco—he was guest in our home when we were still living in northern California—he asserted so strong a distaste for his Germanness that, could he have changed the course of his life, he would have exchanged that identity for another; he seemed near tears when he said that. I was perplexed, and uncomfortable.

By the time we met that night at the bar that faced Alcatraz across the bay, I had gathered further details about the man. One that still stings today was his passing reference to a weekend of great skiing in Bavaria, on the border with Austria. "When was that?" I had asked. "Oh, sometime late in March, back in '38," he said, with no recognition. But I did remember. That week, young men in the same uniform Westphal wore then rampaged through Jewish homes in my town. Several prominent members of the *kehillah* were arrested, beaten, and sent to Dachau; two died there in the following days. And this man who faced me over a glass of beer was in those hours having a lovely week in the snows of the Alps. How could I traverse the icy chasm between us and now talk jazz and bacterial endotoxins and listen to his confession? There were also colleagues in my field who claimed that Westphal had remained more the S.S. man than the laboratory director who protected carriers of genes defined as Jewish by the Nüremberg racial laws. And yet that man had nothing to gain from me but a hearing. The honesty and the sincerity and the pain were real. I had not before come across anything like it, not during my assignment to a military intelligence unit in the U.S. army of occupation in Germany, nor, later, at international scientific gatherings.

I found myself disarmed by Westphal's integrity already at the beginning, when he urged me to come to the Freiburg workshop. I acceded. But I swore myself to a cold professionalism during that week. I would not enjoy the stay, and I would brashly advertise my Jewishness at every opportunity.

In the taxi from the Freiburg airport to the hotel, the driver remarked that the few words of direction I gave him were in perfectly pronounced German, no American accent. That was quite true. Every language I speak is inflected with the *Muttersprache*, and only in German can I pass as a native. I told him that I was an American Jew who had been driven out of the *Heimat* as a child, and I volunteered the information that I was not pleased to find myself back in a German land. He said nothing for a moment, then pulled up to the side of the road, and stripped off his shirt:

"Look!" he said. His back was lacerated from shoulder to hip by a row of deep, parallel scars.

"My credentials, mister," he said. "A souvenir from Buchenwald. Two years."

"Are you Jewish?" I asked.

"Oh, no! Very pure Aryan! But a Socialist."

An introduction to the ambiguity that permeated the rest of that week. Westphal took me into the confidences of his life. I met some of the Jews he had sheltered. I met a senior member of the Institute who had narrowly escaped arrest and execution together with the *Weisse Rose* group which, under the leadership of a young brother and sister, the Scholls, had in the middle of the war distributed leaflets that accused the regime of barbarity in its persecutions of the Jews and urged resistance. There were a few others who told me, with a straightforwardness I could not doubt, that they had opposed the Nazis but were not ready for self-sacrifice. At every meal, care was taken by my hosts that I could dine with them without transgressing the Mosaic dietary laws. I lived largely on fish prepared by immersion in a vat of boiling water —blue trout, a Schwarzwald delicacy. The kindness and the consideration for the comfort of a reluctant guest were overwhelming. But so was the knowledge that I walked in a wasteland. Freiburg once had a flourishing Jewish community. Nothing remained. Had all those who extinguished it simply disappeared, had Sodom and Gomorrah been repopulated by cadres of the righteous? Or had I been set on a temporary, rarefied island of international fellowship, our hosts taking great care that the ambience be one of empathy with the sensibilities of the Jewish colleagues? The scientific discussions were exhilarating, and the ideas that were probed and sifted proved to be a compass point for my work in the coming decades. But I was at peace with myself only on leaving: Back in California, I could once again breathe unambiguous air.

I continued my relationship with Westphal from there, and then from Israel. We collaborated across the ether on several research projects. Westphal and Hans Fischer of the *Weisse Rose* visited my department in Jerusalem and broke bread with my family at our home. But I did not wish to return to Germany, even though that country, unlike Austria, took it upon itself to make reparation and often stood politically at Israel's side.

The second journey to Germany was also prompted by Westphal. His Institute had the custom of celebrating the seventieth birthday of outstanding members by dedicating a symposium and *Festschrift* in their honor. Prominent scholars in the sciences, arts, and humanities read learned papers and the evenings were given over to social galas. At least one Israeli academician was always featured among the lecturers. I was to be that lecturer in 1976; the honoree that year was a man of an old, conservative Catholic family, known to have had no affection for Nazism. For several years preceding, one of my departmental colleagues had been awarded grants from Freiburg for collaborative research. I could not really, I told myself, act out my detachment when the department I led enjoyed support from the Germans.

In my opening remarks, knitted *kippah* on my head, I reflected on the oddities of contingency: But for the grace of God, I declared, German science would have relegated me to ashes at "Labor Auschwitz," as Benno Müller-Hill, science's voice of conscience in postwar Germany, has so aptly termed the capital of that planet of death; and now I stood before them reflecting on nature and science and the ethics that must keep biology and medicine from once more descending into monstrosity, like the "hygiene of race"—*Rassenhygiene*—that had turned German genetics, anthropology, and psychiatry into a *tödliche Wissenschaft*, deadly science. Enthusiastic applause. The audience was predominantly of older gentlemen who had held positions in the war years. I was surrounded after the session, congratulated on the significance of the remarks. *"Sie haben das richtig und mit Gefühl gesagt. Höchst wichtig. . . . Wir freuen uns so das Sie heute mit uns zusammen sind!"*—you spoke the truth, and with real feeling. That is so important. . . . We are so happy you are with us today! The rabbi's son the center of admiration. Drinks. Blue trout. Schnapps after dinner. Conviviality. Despite myself, because of myself, I felt the core of scrupulous antipathy within me melting.

Next morning, a younger man who had stood aloof seated himself beside me at breakfast. There were just the two of us.

"Do you know some of the people who complimented you so nicely last night?" he asked.

"No. Why do you ask?"

He recited a roster of names. Two or three sounded vaguely familiar. My companion explained. This one was involved with Hallervorden. That one with Mengele's laboratory back in Marburg. Those had faced denazification tribunals under the Allied occupation, were found guilty and paid their penalties, and now filled preeminent posts at Germany's universities and research institutes.

"You held strange court," he said.

On the stormy flight home, I took the measure of my convictions and found them appallingly wanting. Friends tried to reassure me. "It's only natural to flow with sympathy. Times change. People change. They were surely sincere with their acclamation." Yes, perhaps, but they had surely been sincere, too, when they were part of the machinery of destruction. I don't care for that kind of flow. I didn't care for myself. The flaw was not merely circumstantial, it went deeper. I was the proud Jew who cannot keep his tail from wagging when admitted to the club. Well, if that was my pride's mettle, I would not, ever again, put myself to the test. *Nunc mas.*

And then came the call to a ceremonial occasion in Vienna. I did not go. The others did. I was criticized by some of them, and by members of my own department, for intransigence, for a vindictiveness whose time had passed. I knew better, how thin and wavering a component of my character constancy is. I knew that my not going was more a thing of preemptive defense against myself. And I like my principled animosities unconditional, clean and impervious to a soft moment's irresolution. The exchange with the Austrians found its way, with their concurrence, into the pages of an American Jewish journal. I was glad of that and of the criticism, some of which was also published there. I was on record. I could not anonymously vacillate again.

And now, suddenly, there materialize the Eiwens, with all their encompassing earnestness and love. I explained, slowly and with great care, that a return to Wr. Neustadt would be not only emotionally wracking for me but also quite impossible. I tell them about Freiburg and about the overture from the Austrian immunologists that I had turned down, my refusal enshrined in print, a totemic deterrent to equivocation. "Have you then never been back to your hometown?" Uli wanted to know. Well, as a matter of fact, I had, but the circumstances then had been very different and if they had involved any fortitude on my part it was of a different, uncompromising kind.

Chapter 5

GUARDIAN ANGEL
AS *STARSHINA*

Oberursel, near Frankfurt. Supreme Headquarters Allied Expeditionary Forces, European Command Intelligence Center. I am nineteen years old, a private in an interrogation unit of the U.S. army of occupation. Most of the others in the outfit are, like me, youngsters of European origin who had found refuge and a new citizenship in America and enlisted on reaching age. Many of us are Jewish. We were selected for this assignment because we speak foreign languages, scored reasonably well on the army's version of IQ tests, and had a year or two of college. We had basic infantry training, several months of a military intelligence cram course in the States or in the idyllic Alpine setting of Oberammergau, and then we were turned loose as interrogator-investigators.

We wear officer's olive greens on the job, without insignia. The uniform is to give us standing when we confront our clients, men twice our age or more who held field-grade ranks in the S.S. and are imprisoned on charges of crimes against humanity or on suspicion of membership in "Werewolf" groups, as they call themselves, who plan terrorist actions against the occupying forces. We study the top-secret files on each suspect, record and analyze their talk among themselves in their wired cells and, once the outlines of a case can be discerned, begin the interrogations. Armed guards bring the prisoners to the offices in which each one of us sits, alone. One on one. The guards wait outside, and should the need arise can be alerted by pressing a button at our fingertips.

I feel totally unequipped. The disparity of age, experience, and rank

is too great. How to cut through the endless protestations of innocence, the labyrinthine explanations? The lieutenant colonel who was
sentenced to death in absentia by a Yugoslav court for the murder of
Serbs and Jews was, he swore, a philo-Semite; he had shed tears when
on *Kristallnacht* the synagogue in his town was razed; the list of names
sewn into the lining of his jacket was of friends who were forming a
dance club. The S.S. major was assigned to the battalion against his will;
he had carried out no function more reprehensible than that of quarter-
master. Physical persuasion is not permitted at the center. The pressures
we can bring to bear are trivial, cancellation of mail and visitor privileges, a restricted diet, that sort of thing. Our tools of the trade are our
brains. Yes, but most of us are still very wet behind the ears. The colonel
finally breaks when his addiction is discovered and his supply of heroin-
laced cookies from home is peremptorily interrupted. The major, a Ba-
varian, says too much one night in a moment of anger when his cellmate,
a Prussian Gestapo man, taunts him for sloppiness in the performance of
his duties in Poland; he makes his admission when the recording is
played back to him. The accomplishments owe nothing to my investiga-
tive skills.

   The army, in its renowned wisdom, adds a measure of schizophrenia
to our stark immaturity. Our daytime working hours are supervised by
civilized men, civilian employees who had seen service in the O.S.S. and
other intelligence branches. Back in our barracks, we precocious professionals fall into the hands of noncommissioned regulars who despise
with a vengeance the uppity foreign pretenders in officer's camouflage.
Fatigues, KP, latrine duty, ferocious inspections. No leave for weeks at a
time (the unintended benefit of the restriction was enforced disengage-
ment from the numerous Fräuleins of all social classes who could be
rented for the price of a pack of PX cigarettes). I live through nearly a
year of this, dissembling and blustering. I achieve a *modus vivendi* with a
particularly offensive sergeant major when I do well at the rifle range
and, to his puzzled inquiry, "How come a fucking intellectual can hold a
gun?" assure him that my fucking way of speaking has no roots in any
pretensions of the intellect but only in an unfortunate impairment of the
vocal chords. "Oh," he bellows "so you're a bit of a soldier, after all!"
When assigned to weekend guard duty in the tower overlooking the
prison stockade, I loudly let it be known that with the M–1 in my hands
I would shoot as many damned Krauts as there are bullets in the clip. I

do nothing of the sort, of course. European Jews vigorously adopted the restraints of civilized behavior that our gentile compatriots had treated so lightly.

Reprieve. My request to the Red Cross and army authorities for a compassionate leave to Vienna has come through, to see my grandmother in an old-age home. It requires special permission to get into the city from American-occupied Germany, across the Russian zones of occupation. Incredibly, Rosa Kohn had survived nearly three years of Theresienstadt. She was a prissy, delicate old lady, and my sister and I had greeted her periodic incursions into our childhood home with considerable ambivalence. Playing noisily in Omama's earshot was taboo. Rosa Kohn had fainting spells when she was disturbed. She could only tolerate eggs laid a few hours before they were boiled for precisely two minutes and thirty seconds; the rest of her diet had to be equally safeguarded from staleness, contamination, and a variety of other imagined blemishes. Sickly for most of her life, she had cast the spell of her infirmities over her husband, who died in the influenza pandemic that swept the land in the early 1920s, and then over the families of her children. I grew up on legendary stories of the devotion due and paid to the stricken lady. When only in her forties, she could no longer manage the flights of stairs that led to her apartment in the capital, and once a month her husband carried her in his arms to the *mikveh* some distance away for the prescribed ablution after her period. When he lacked the strength for that, he, devoutly orthodox observer of the Law that he was, refrained for nearly two decades before his death from conjugal contact with her. But he adored her all the same, we children were told; they should be a model to us of conjugal love in the ways of the Torah. Our mother who, at least in memory, worshipped her famous artist father, *Kaiserlich-Königlicher Hofmaler* to the court of Franz Josef I, lived in the dread of filial piety owed her mother. Owed her, moreover, was a sympathetic understanding of the gloom in which she had encased herself. She had lost four children to childhood diseases before a son and a daughter made it into adulthood. She was deported in 1942. A high Gestapo official with monarchist leanings who had been a schoolmate of her son apparently saw to it that her number was expunged from the records upon her arrival in Theresienstadt. Unlike almost everyone else in that one "model" camp, she was not sent on to Auschwitz. As a person without a recorded identity, she triumphed there over the tumult of bedlam and deprivation and rode back to Vienna on the back of a Russian armored vehicle in the spring of 1945. Rosa Kohn was eighty-one years old when she walked into the home on the Seegasse.

I am the first to be with my grandmother again. When I enter the ward, an old woman rises from a chair to greet me. I think this is my grandmother. But I am mistaken. The woman leads me to a bed down the corridor, and then I recognize her, wizened and feeble but lucid. The only one of my own who has been in the fire and come through.

My grandmother does not speak of her deportation and the years in Theresienstadt. Is it reticence, or, after all, the capriciousness of memory's hold? I can't tell. She grasps my forearm tightly—the bony fingers are surprisingly strong—and talks of good times long ago, of family and the small things that made up the weave of her life before she was hurried down the flights of her Vienna house and pushed into a dark-green van for the first lap of the journey to the concentration camp.

When I come back the next day, she has a gift for me, a small plastic folder with a few bills. Concentration camp script, KZ money, she tells me.

I am no longer able to recall the particulars of what we said to each other, only the agitation I felt, the equivocal recollections of childhood giving way to a flood of affection and to the sense of something precious recovered.

The hours I am not with her I spend with Rosa Nassau. A Catholic of peasant background, she kept her Jewish husband hidden in an attic throughout the long years of persecution. The Nassaus were family friends; I regard her as an aunt. She is a firebrand, taunting the shop-keepers in the neighborhood for their Nazi enthusiasm, which they now loudly disclaim. She understands the request I make of her, although she tries hard to dissuade me.

I need civilian clothes so I can make my way to Wr. Neustadt, some fifty kilometers southwest of the city. It is a risky business. Wr. Neustadt is Russian military headquarters and strictly off limits to Americans. It has been made very clear to us by our commanding officer that should we stray into Russian lines and be caught the intelligence services would deny our existence; the Cold War had begun, and the army wants no unnecessary altercations with the Soviets. I have no Austrian papers, and I know perfectly well the policy of all four occupying forces: In any contact with civilians, identification documents are demanded at once.

This is in order to curb infiltration by intelligence agents and by the black marketeers who flourish amidst the chaos of the conquered Axis nations. A lack of papers means arrest on the spot, and under less than gentlemanly interrogation it would not take long to discover that I am not an Austrian lost on his way home.

But the impulse to be back for a few hours in my hometown is overwhelming. I have had recurrent dreams for years of walking its streets just one more time, of seeing its houses and the trees in the *Akademie* park where we used to roam. The draw is atavistic, despite all the bitterness that went with the ejection from childhood and the knowledge of the alternative that had awaited those who couldn't escape. I do not really comprehend the urge but neither can I resist it.

I do something terribly foolish. In shabby slacks and a leather jacket provided by Rosa Nassau, I take the train to Wr. Neustadt. When I leave the station I recognize nothing. The town is a shambles. Later that day I am told that it was the most heavily bombed town in the country; there had been a Messerschmidt factory there. At this moment I see only rubble that obscures any familiarity that the blasted streets might have conveyed. I turn to a passerby and ask for directions to the Volksbadgasse, on the outskirts, where Mina Gneist lives. The need to hold Mina's hand is as great as that of again holding the town in my eyes, to fix it firmly in memory, confirm that it really had been.

The passerby is friendly. "I can't help you," he says, "I am from Linz. Can't find the way through this bloody pile myself. But I'll take you to someone who can."

And with that I am grasped by the arm and steered through the entrance of the half-ruined building at which we stand. Before me, very close, sits a man behind a desk raised a step up above the sawdust-littered floor. The room is lit by a single weak electric bulb, bare but for a photograph of Stalin pasted onto the wall above the podium. The sitting man is a *starshina* of the Russian military police. There is an aroma of garlic and vodka. My guide says: "This fellow is lost. He wants the Volksbadgasse." The sergeant nods indifferently, sets his tumbler down, walks over and hustles me out the door, and with a convivial pat on the shoulder gives me my bearings. Not a word is exchanged between us. Outside, I find myself shaking. Had he asked me anything, would I now be on the way to Siberia? Or to where?

A painting that I liked as a child flashes before me. It is of a rosy-faced little girl, hand in hand with her smaller brother, crossing a rotten, rickety bridge over a wild torrent. Behind them with wings outspread and hands almost touching their shoulders hovers a smiling guardian angel. I had seen that picture in many of the neighboring farmhouses and I had hoped such an angel would float behind me, too.

Many years later, my friend Pater Johannes Vrbecky expressed the thought that guardian angels sometimes come in the guise of a Russian policeman.

I went back to Austria twice more in the following years to be with Mina and Rosa Nassau. When they died, I resolved to close the book. The apotheosis of recollection was done with, the town, beautifully rebuilt in its medieval form, would forever be no more than the scorched earth its brown-shirted *Bürgers* had made of it for me. The dreams stopped. Only the nightmare remained.

No return.

Chapter 6

ROOTS AND SPECTERS

A nd suddenly, here in Jerusalem, the home that had always been, long before I set foot in it, the Eiwens appear, from nowhere, and pry at the bindings of the volume whose last page I had wished done and sealed.

One should not revisit cloudlands and surely not the eye of a storm. But my reluctance goes far deeper than that common wisdom. To have the minutes of my meetings with myself reopened, laid bare to glaring scrutiny, would do violence to the persona I desperately seek to perceive in the mirror of self-reflection. I must see myself as unflinching in moments of truth, moments when shrinking back from resolve would earn me the white feather of cowardice.

The terror of showing vacillation, even if only to myself, is irreversibly woven into my being. The thread runs absurdly through everything I think and do, and each imagined confrontation looms before me as if the history of encounters with myself had only then begun, as if there were no log of challenges overcome to be found in the archives of the mind.

Perhaps that terror is idiosyncratic, perhaps it, too, is a legacy of childhood's song in a strange land.

We children were, I think, more acutely aware than our parents of the bimodality of Jewish existence between World War I and the Anschluss. Adults more glibly rationalize and compromise, they come to grips with their situation. The universities were open. Jews were prominent in commerce, medicine, the law. If Jewish students were periodically the targets of rioting defenders of collegiate Aryan purity, workmen's guilds barred, the clubs and halls of society largely restricted, and anti-Semitism ever so often blared from ecclesiastic and political podiums, why, all that paled when viewed against the economic and physical persecutions in the East. Blood libel and pogrom were still fresh in the dark iconography of European Jews, and the level of security we thought finally to have attained in countries of the West was exhilarating. The adults focused on the half cup that was full, and greeted each added drop as validation of the messianic dream of reason and enlightenment among all the nations on earth.

How patriotic we were, how confident of our deep anchorage in Austria's soil! Roots. The names of the places where my mother's people had lived for the past two centuries—she couldn't trace the line back to before the early 1700s—still ring in my ears like a litany deeply imprinted: Tulln, Baden-bei-Wien, Wien, Klosterneuburg, Vöslau, St. Pölten, Trautmannsdorf. There her father was born, there her grandfather and great-grandfather had been rabbis, and generations before them tradesmen and managers of noblemen's estates.

Luminous memories. The Crown Prince Erzherzog Rainer, visiting her father's summer cottage in Baden with an escort of forty mounted officers, to share the Sabbath's traditional third meal. Grandmother's prized possession, a large brooch with the letters in diamonds, *"In Hochachtung und Freundschaft, FJI zu DK."*—in esteem and friendship, FJI to DK. I have handwritten notes between the Kaiser and the painter, arranging portrait sittings, and about other things; *"Erlauchte Majestät . . . ," "Mein geehrter Freund, David . . ."* Family icons. When David Kohn postponed a sitting because the date fell on the intermediary days of the Sukkoth festival, the Kaiser expressed admiration for his religious steadfastness. In a recent book of reminiscences by the Kaiser's Chamberlain there is a passage in which the Kaiser muses, "Maler Kohn is not only a great artist but also a great man!"

When he wasn't painting the court aristocracy, the royal artist did exquisite pastels—in Rötel—of the elders at the *Kapishnitzer Hasidic stibl* where three times daily he made his devotions. His family's circumstances were modest, below his means. The money earned from his commissions went to found a home for children orphaned in the pogroms that ravaged Galicia when the monarchy lost its hold in the East.

I have met elderly men and women who knew my grandfather,

who stare at me in awe when they learn that the name I carry is his—glory transgenerationally reflected—and recall his walking the streets of Vienna, the patrician figure with the "penetrating eyes that saw all," the supplicant soliciting contributions door to door for his *Waisenhaus*. I sat one day at a table in a restaurant in London's Soho, reading a paper and waiting for the soup I had ordered. The waitress approached, I lifted my face and she froze, dropping the bowl. "You are the *Enkelkind* of Maler Kohn," she managed to whisper. "You must be! You have his eyes! Are you, really?" I assured her I am. As an orphaned girl, she had helped him distribute soup among the children. "He was such a majestic man," she said.

My father's family were from across the border, Pressburg, Suranyi. They, too, had been natives of the region for several hundred years. His father's grocery store on the Judengasse below the *Schloss* was half as large as my narrow office in Jerusalem. The merchandise consisted mainly of the contents of a few wooden tubs, salted fish called "Russians," povidl jam, rock salt, flour. When enough had been earned to make ends meet for that day and the next, Moshe Weiss retreated to his volumes in the small wooden prayer house on the courtyard's far side, the Weiss *Shul*. Scholars and students came from all over Central Europe for his *halachic* expositions. His wife's grandfather, Ephraim Fischel Sussman Sofer, was *dayan*—arbiter—of the rabbinic court of the Chatam Sofer, the nineteenth century's foremost authority in Orthodox Judaism in the lands west of Poland. Ephraim Sofer's sons and grandsons founded a rabbinic dynasty, the Sofrim, whose works on law and *midrash* are on the bookshelves of my study.

I had my first lessons in *Mishnah* from my grandfather when I was six. He chose a tractate that dealt with priestly ritual at the Temple, because my other, *Kaiserlich-Königlicher* grandfather was a *Kohen*.

My father studied at Pressburg's Chatam Sofer *yeshivah*. He was regarded as an *ilui*, a prodigy, but he was thrown out, his illustrious antecedents notwithstanding, when Latin and Greek grammar books were discovered hidden in his closet. Secular learning was a short road to apostasy. He continued to study, alone, in both worlds. When the First World War broke out, he enlisted in a Honved Hussar regiment and served for four years with distinction as company commander and field chaplain on the Eastern front. His variegated education came in good stead there. When the regiment's Christian chaplains had fallen, he knew what to speak at the side of dying Christian and Muslim soldiers. He was very proud of the medals he was awarded.

When the war ended and authority in the eastern reaches of the Empire lapsed into a vacuum, Slovak peasants massed at the gates of Pressburg's Jewish quarter on the eve of Passover. A blood libel accusation, spring 1919. The *yeshivah* declared a fast and penitential prayers. My father also fasted, but as he fasted he hurriedly assembled a group of other Jewish veterans. They broke into an armory and commandeered four machine guns, two for each of the main portals to the ghetto. When the mob came, they fired. There was no pogrom that Passover in Pressburg. The *yeshivah* considered this to be a further outrage, a taking of fate out of God's hands into human. My father, so I was told by comrades in arms who came to *shivah* when he died in 1954, argued the case of Deborah and Yael, the Maccabees, Akivah and Bar Kochba's revolt against the Romans. To no avail. He took things into his hands. That was what the Greek and Roman classics taught, not the sages of Chatam Sofer. He was grudgingly forgiven only when he married the daughter of Maler Kohn, whose orthodox credentials, despite the painting, could not be faulted even by Chatam Sofer standards.

Heinrich Hillel Weiss went on to a doctorate in history from Vienna and to the rabbinate of Wr. Neustadt and Neunkirchen. He was an imposing presence, with his charcoal beard and silver-handled cane, clothed in the black frock and Roman collar that was the garb of Austrian rabbis as well as of the Christian clergy. People made way for him. He commanded respect in the town, and he was loved by his congregants. An inspired educator, he taught semitics at the classical high school and was appointed professor and inspector of religious education in the *Landesschulrat*, the Ministry of Education of Niederösterreich. Within a few years he had achieved a position of authority and leadership among Austria's Jews. Shortly before the Anschluss, he was called to the pulpit of the preeminent orthodox congregation in Vienna. He declined the offer; the sanctuary's seating arrangements for men and women did not meet his own *halachic* standards.

I, his only son, sometimes feel as if there were resting on my skull the apex of an inverted triangle of family descent, the lines of monarchichal and rabbinic glory converging to a point and pressing; I owe that paradigm of intimidating patrimony to St. Clair McKelway's depiction of *his* sense of pedigree from generations of stern New England Protestant divines.

Roots.

Mine are not as maverick as they might seem today. In that brief watershed of modern European history, worlds met, cultures intercalated. There was hope of a brave new era of synthesis. There were also lines of stress, sunken below the surface of things one wished to behold, but they emerged at moments when euphoria and its lurking denouements could not quite easily be teased apart.

I grew up with all that. I grew up as a Jew in the full meaning of the word; and I grew up a wildly patriotic Austrian. When I was still very small, I would salute every passing lorry of soldiers and when one would wave the flag in acknowledgment my day was made. There was no Jewish school in town, I was given private lessons in prayer book and scripture, and the teacher realized that the biblical tales of battle and salvation would best be absorbed when I was permitted to play them out with lead soldiers, brave Austrian infantry under Obergeneral Moses and Lieutenant-General Aharon beating back Amalek's hordes.

But I grew up as well in another, parallel dimension.

I already then was drawn to the outdoors, to open spaces and animals, and among my earliest recollections are walks with my mother in knee-deep snow through fields to take food to starving squirrels and birds. At six, my mother took me to enroll in the Animal Welfare Society and I learned from an embarrassedly smiling gentleman that there was a problem; it would be . . . ah . . . a good idea if Jewish parents would found such a group for *their* children.

School was difficult. The professor who taught German language in the first grade of high school occasionally called the class to order with the proclamation, "Boys, shape up, this is not a Jew school!" We were two Jewish children among nearly forty. Gym was worse. It was said that the Nazi movement was the uprising of physical education instructors; these were embittered men who had lost their military commissions with the monarchy's defeat at the hands of the international "communist-capitalist cabal" and who entered their new profession as a stopgap until a greater Germany would once again recognize their worthiness. Jewish children were often the butt of ridicule when they were slow on the ropes, and parents would obtain certification of nonexistent frailties to have them released. The taunt *"Saujud"* from an annoyed playmate or passerby should have been ignored, par for the course as it was, and my father suggested that I return the compliment,

"Yea, I am the Jew, you are the swine," and sometimes I did, but it cut because it split identity: Was I, in fact, only the still scorned Jew? Was I not also the scion of royalty? I could not differentiate between the status of those born to royalty and those who served it, but that confusion was to an extent, if more subtly, also my family's.

There were the funeral corteges, priests and acolytes in pagan vestment escorting the black hearse with black-plumed horses that brought the heathen in his coffin to eternal judgment before the crucified bleeding rabbi, *Rex Judeorum* they called him, but he was not mine; bystanders along the way must kneel, and I would run to find a doorway hiding place because a Jew bends knee only before the King of Kings. The thronged processions of Corpus Christi, of martyred saints on their days, monstrance and effigies of painted plaster and thorn-wreathed crosses held aloft to the sun, Roman legions marching with crests and banners, hep, hep, *Hyerosolima est perdita*—Jerusalem is lost, the peasants streaming into town exultant with piety and schnapps, *Dies Irae*, and we knew, we knew, that we were Christ's killers and closed the shutters.

It seems to me that beyond a certain age, children are in some ways anchored in the real world more unerringly than adults, are more receptive to both its overt and subliminal signals. Children usually know the points of departure and return when they are transported to realms of the imagination. But here were crassly conflicting realities, in the here and now. I could not reconcile them, and so I tried to find a firmer ground of identity in fantasies.

I would pore over the picture, camels and palm trees, on the oval wooden containers in which dates were packaged—Purim gifts bought by family friends at Leonardo's, the town's Italian greengrocer—and long for Palestina. But that was clearly a very distant dreamland. It did leave its mark, though. Thirty years later I felt impelled to relinquish a gilded California existence for the uncertainties of Israel. But then, in Wr. Neustadt, the fantasy was only that, not a real escape from reality's conflicts.

There was another route. I devoured the adventure stories of Karl May, and later the sagas of the American frontiersman and cowboy. From them I learned what a young man must be. Strong, intrepid, valiant. Courage never fails a man who would call himself man. That message struck a deep chord of frustration. I took it back with me into the split real world. It was reinforced, in retrospect perhaps not so surprisingly, by what I now prefer to regard as an offhand, thoughtless remark of my father's one day when I came home from school, upset. Some rough street brats had jeered and jostled me. Father asked, absentmindedly, "You gave it back to them properly, right?" No, I had hesitated, shrunk back. Father exclaimed, impatiently, "Ah, don't be such a *Hasenfuss!*" A rabbit's foot, a runner. Rabbit, don't run. The sentence rang and rang and has echoed down the years. Rabbit don't run. Ever. Never. You can't live it down if you falter. My father was the heroic paragon. In my teens I recognized him on occasion in less gallant postures, excessively flattering before a uniform, an American immigration official, a brusque bus driver, kowtowing. But in the mind's recesses the pedestal remained intact. I can forgive myself no weakness, no indecision, real or nightmarish. When I found out that Karl May was also Adolf Hitler's favorite writer, that made no difference either.

I have jogged for most of adult life, often to exhaustion. Rabbit permits himself to run, he escapes the verdict; for *that* running he wins acclaim, "Six miles? At your age! What strength!" Rabbit must always overcome. I was afraid of little dogs that barked, and I have helped a ranger in the Timbavati catch twelve-foot mambas with bare hands and a stick. In the Kaokoland desert, the young Afrikaner woman with me says: "You could get quite close to them, you know, if you aren't scared!" and I leave her behind in the Land Rover and crawl through the sand on my stomach to the cover of a scraggly thornbush a few yards away from a herd of Namib elephants. I was terrified of heights, and I fly in microlights over Moremi and Savuti plains tracing animal migrations. With success and recognition within my grasp, I have left terrains of science and continents to start all over again. And more and more, ad nauseam. The unrequited fear of striking back with fists. Oh, yes, I have done that, too, laid out a Hitler Jugend bully on the oiled classroom floor, wrestled a Boston Irish tough to the barracks floor in boot camp, but there were always others to be fought, so many. For every challenge met, there have been so many others I have not.

I turned to the tried, ultimate Jewish weapon of rationality, reasoned argument. I have reasoned myself out of many tight corners, talked opponents into friendship, am said to be cocky and daring, and that leaves only a bitter taste in my mouth. That is not manliness. The savior of Pressburg and Karl May would have done it otherwise.

It has been an interesting life, pursued by specters of fear and brav-
ery. And now the Eiwens, and I am very much afraid to return. Back to
the place that had despised me, that I despise? Another retreat from
fortitude?

Chapter 7

THE TACTICS OF REMEMBRANCE

I know only too well the overwhelming need to be accepted, a need that was not fulfilled in the place and time of my youth. It is still an overcoming for me to stand out in a crowd. It is with a gritting of teeth that I wear the *kippah* or don *tefillin* in public places in gentile space. Earlier in my career, I quaked for days before delivering a lecture. In the overcoming I become the admired teacher, seemingly relaxed and full of self-confidence; few know the agonizing hours of preparation that go into an hour's talk, even on the same subject, the same course, year after year. I have cultivated, in dress and demeanor, the manners of one who doesn't give a damn for what is thought correct. But beneath all the savoir faire the need simmers and sometimes it breaks out shamefully.

As the only Jewish kid in the platoon at basic training, fresh out of *yeshivah*, it took a while to win admittance as a regular guy to the group of kids from small Georgia towns and Boston slums. The only Jew in the unit, I was eventually forgiven that religious clanship, even the attendance at chapel on Friday nights when the barracks were in turmoil preparing for Saturday morning's white-glove inspection; I reciprocated the tolerance, volunteering for KP on Sundays and Christian holy days. But then, in the middle of training, Percy was transferred to us from another platoon. Percy. Not a regular guy's name, surely, and not really a regular guy. Clumsy with the rifle, bookish, a loner, prissy. Within days, he was given a nickname: faggot. Percy was taunted relentlessly. Percy suffered. And, yes, Percy was a Jew. He looked to me for companionship, for moments of reprieve from the exclusion and hazing. And I, I was mortified and frightened. I wanted no commonness between us, no stigma by association, no undermining of my hard-won status. I kept Percy at a distance. One morning, as the company was breaking up on the parade grounds after reveille, I mockingly mewed after him in high falsetto. The guys laughed approvingly. Percy stared at me, unbelieving. "You, too?" he said, and walked away. He did not speak to me again, and when later in the day I mumbled an apology he walked away. A passage in the Talmud has it that embarrassing someone in front of others is one of the few wrongdoings for which forgiveness is not granted. The gates of repentance are closed, the world to come is barred. I had known that. But for me, it seems, the need for social acceptance can be addictive, and when my guard is down for a moment I might sell out redemption itself for less than the weight of thirty talents.

Now, with the Eiwens, I am very much on guard. To be handed the forbidden apple of belonging at the source of its archetypic withholding might be more of a temptation than I can overcome.

How to avoid the challenge? On the grounds of emotional discomfort? That would be a spineless running away. I take refuge once again in reason that evening around the Sabbath table, and after they have returned to Austria reason is my defense in the intensive exchange of letters that follows.

I am very sympathetic, I declare, to their sense of collective responsibility for Christianity's long persecutions. To admit to wrongdoing, to make amends and seek forgiveness, is the way of redemption in Judaism too. It is *tshuvah*—sincere repentance—that narrows the distance between the human and the divine. Forgiveness for transgressions between man and man can be implored of God only after it has been entreated of the persons wronged. In the days before Yom Kippur—the solemn day of atonement—we must seek out those we have hurt and pledge remorse and restitution; if the plea is repulsed, it must be repeated, humbly, facing a *minyan*—a quorum—of the community. Only then can God be offered contrition for transgressions against Him.

But I am not the right address for Helmuth and Uli and Ichthys. *They* have done me no evil. They have wronged no Jew. And I am not EveryJew. I cannot speak for the Six Million nor for those before them: no one among the living can grant absolution. When the victim no longer exists, the surrogacy of repentance is heaven's. Surely the Eiwens must understand that.

They do, of course. It had not occurred to them, they respond, to perceive me as a mediator. They regard me as "an individual, a Jew who has himself suffered our nation's anti-Semitism and to whom we are charged to express, face to face and in the place in which this great wrong was done, how deeply in our heart remorse is engraved." They see themselves as *Nachkommer*—descendants—of those who as Christians sinned, and as Christians they themselves stand accused if they do not before God and man shoulder the conscience of other generations, the conscience that was shrugged off by their fathers. And as that conscience is burdened by the enormities of a hatred that threatened the very existence of the Jewish people, their cry of shame, of guilt deferred, must ring commensurately unambiguous before the world.

And I, too, have taken on a charge, I reply. I write of the sacrament of memory. The Baal Shem Tov, the eighteenth-century founder of Hasidism, put it succinctly: "In memory lies salvation." The words are engraved on the portals of *Yad Vashem*. Memory has dimmed. Half a century later, forgetfulness is settling over the fate that befell European Jewry. Many of the younger generation barely know what took place. Many do not wish to know. Voices are raised that would altogether deny the reality of the Holocaust. Some who do remember marginalize it as just one other unavoidable consequence of war, one among countless violent episodes that go with conflict, but it's over now, life moves on, we must get back to the matters at hand. *Lupus est homo homini, non homo*—wolf, not human, is man to other men . . . that's how we are, there have always been regrettable things we've done to one another. No cause, though, to be all that obsessive about what happened to some Jews fifty years ago! Many more people perished in the Gulag, and how many German civilians in their razed cities? The Holocaust should be seen in balanced perspective, an unfortunate by-play in the grand scenario of the struggle between East and West. . . . There are Jews, too, who prefer the sliding into amnesia. There is ease in Lethe. It is a very human thing to forget, it is required for the normal disposition of society. But human society cannot claim normalcy after the Holocaust. And forgetfulness carries a mortally dangerous edge. It blurs distinctions between gradations of prejudice and malevolence, between gradations of responsibility. It paves a smoothly traveled path toward an endlessness of monstrous inhumanities. The Holocaust must be chiseled into the mileposts at the far reaches of human sentience. It marks how far and how fast "civilized" nations can race into barbarity; how great the price of indifference; and, too, how some men and women can marshal the courage to resist.

It is not eternal hatred and vengeance that I wish to advocate, I tell the Eiwens. When I demand remembrance it is, rather, to cry out against the soporific comforts of denial, against the facile coming to peace with the lupine in our nature. As if we had no choice, as if there were not other potentials. Fashioned as we may have been in the divine image, we all too easily shed that image and render service to that Other that surely confuses even Lucifer . . . one million children . . . but we are not programmed to such service. We know also to string pearls of light for the delight of heaven. I have enlisted in the cause of memory so that when we stand before other points of no return we might recall, and tremble, and pause, and grant ourselves loopholes of escape from the wolf. What that enlistment implies for me is a declarative distancing from the collectivity of the hordes who brought this new darkness into the world. It is a very small, symbolic gesture, a statement that time must slow. Not everything may fade so quickly, some things must stand longer, beacons of warning.

But that high-flown epistle could make no converts. The Eiwens are already committed. It is only in the tactics of remembrance that we differ, and as I read their reply I find myself disarmed: Their tactics are better. We would be returning to Wr. Neustadt not in anonymity, not as tourists but as *Zeitzeugen*, witnesses to an era. *"Allein schon Eure Anwesenheit in Wr. Neustadt hätte eine Funktion des Wachrüttelns . . ."*—your very presence in Wr. Neustadt would be a shaking up of memory, of a knowing that has been swept under the rug. The *Woche der Begegnung* could well force a process of recall, a thrust into a confrontation with the past.

So in the end I am defenseless. The argument of reason backfires. And the Christianity of the Eiwens is one not estranged from empathy. They will not insist, they understand that the rationality overlays a deep emotional turmoil; they have sensed this, too, from the other Wr. Neustadt survivors with whom I had placed them in contact. The Eiwens know a very different language of *agape* and grace, a language that leaves me vulnerable.

Helmuth and Uli ask only for an opportunity to meet those of us who live in Israel. They want to know us personally, to hear our stories, each one of us, they want to tell us theirs, what brought them to this intersection with *shearith ha'pletah*, the remnants of the destruction.

Most of us live in Jerusalem and in Tel Aviv and its stretches into the Sharon Valley, a smaller number up north, around Haifa and in the Emek Yezreel. I speak with Robert Blum of Kiryath Motzkin. I knew that many close members of his family survived the harsh British internment in Mauritius of Jewish refugees who had managed to reach the shores of Palestine when the Germans overran Europe. Robert is willing to arrange for a get-together of the northerners with the Ichthys group somewhere in the Galilee; we from the south will meet them at a hotel in Jerusalem.

I was already acquainted with most of the Israeli Wr. Neustädters. During Chanukah of 1991, Yaakov Feldman of Yehud and Yehudith Gross, a member of a small religious kibbutz, Beeroth Yitzchak, off Petach Tikvah, organized a reunion in the social room of the kibbutz. Both older than I, they had formed closer friendships with our town's Jewish children and had remained in touch with those who made their way to this country. I had known Yehudith Gross as Lily Schischa. Schischa means "six" in Hebrew; a Sephardi family with six sons had apparently settled in the mid-nineteenth century in the Burgenland, in one of the Seven Towns—the *Sheva Kehilloth*—and the patronym Six devolved on them. That Chanukah night was stormy, roads were flooded, not everyone arrived, but as I entered the room I felt myself propelled as if through some fantastic time warp into the yard of my father's *Tempel* on the Baumkirchnerring and onto the snowy slopes of the Rodelberg in the Stadtpark.

In my mind's eye children are playing. The sleds race down the hill. The flag over the Franz Josef memorial in the park is red-white-red. I run after the older kids, wanting to join in. But now they stand around me, aging men and women, drinking punch and speaking Hebrew and *niederösterreichisches Deutsch*. The flag hanging on the far wall over the table with drinks and snacks is blue-white-blue. A man walks towards me, arms outstretched. I say: "My God, it's you, Walter!" and he embraces me. We have not seen each other since April or May 1938, Walter David Riegler and I. And the others. Fritz and Ernstl Hacker, now Shmuel and Shlomo Givon, the Max-and-Moritz teenagers of my youth. Shlomo, a member of Kibbutz Haogen, has painted a picture of our

Tempel from memory and a faded photograph; he presents me with a copy. Gerstl, Bauer, Zimmer, Breuer, Beinhacker, Yakobovitz, Blum, Bartfeld, Reininger, Jaul . . . the names are the demography of the Jews of the Seven Towns in which most of the Wr. Neustadt community had its roots. Today they are Hebraicized . . . Netzer, Uzzieli, Zur, Matar, Yaron, Segal, Shifrin . . . an overlapping topography of old-new identities. And I am once more Schatzi, the Oberrabbiner's son who is known better by them, the older kids, than he knows them, known less by his cognomen of Little Treasure than as the Little Brat who from the shelter of rabbinic coattails sometimes got away with murder. . . . And more than half a century's distancing seems to have evaporated.

Since that evening at Beeroth Yitzchak we have written and talked to each other. I have told them of the Eiwens and their outlandish beliefs, of a *Woche der Begegnung* that is to be. Many of them have urged me not to fall for this charade . . . a facile playacting of Christian guilt, confession, and absolution . . . a farce, a whitewashing, so much too late. . . . Where were they then when we needed them for our lives, when they might have made a difference. . . . A few were bemusedly sympathetic to the good will, the intent, but certainly, no, they are not going back for any *Begegnung* . . . out of the question. Some have been back, privately, anonymously, to family graves in Wr. Neustadt and the Burgenland, and that was hard enough. I share their feelings precisely. Since I visited Mina Gneist and Rosa Nassau I have not been back at all. For me there are no graves to visit. My parents are buried in New York, and the graves of my grandparents in Vienna's *Zentralfriedhof* do not exert enough of a pull to bring me back to the Austria that has been turned into a vast graveyard of the people to which I belong. I am not acting as emissary or advocate to the Eiwens. I think it only right to show these extraordinary people hospitality in our land and the courtesy of hearing what they wish so fervently to say to us. With some hesitation the Wr. Neustädters agree to make their acquaintance . . . but there should be no misunderstanding. I must tell Helmuth and Uli in advance that their minds are made up. . . . The only *Begegnung* would be in Israel. So we are all of the same mind, and so I write to the pastor and his wife.

Chapter 8

ENCOUNTER AT THE HOLYLAND

FEBRUARY 15, 1995, THE HOLYLAND HOTEL, JERUSALEM

One drives up a winding path from the road that connects the inner city with the Hadassah Medical Center on the outskirts, past a scale model of Jerusalem in the late period of the Second Temple, to arrive at a small plaza on to which the hotel opens. The bare hills on the horizon to the east, only a few kilometers away, were Jordanian territory before the Six Day War.

The lobby is full of people speaking in the soft German dialects of Austria. My active vocabulary is meager—I have had only sporadic occasion to use German since my parents died more than thirty-five years ago—but I have no difficulty understanding the *Muttersprache*. The Ichthys *Gemeinde* is here, over a hundred strong, men, women, and children of all ages. A few other tourists, and the dozen and a half of us Israelis who were once Wr. Neustädters. We are reserved. The only ones I know among the visitors are the Eiwens; the others of our party have met none of them. But beyond the usual awkwardness of first meetings and introductions, we are on guard. We know that these people have come to us full of good will, that most of them were children at the time of the Anschluss or were born after the war, but they are Austrians, and the expressions, the language, the small talk echo back to those of other ordinary men and women who one day not so very long ago donned jackboots and uniforms of brown and black and descended on us with greater ferocity than Ezekiel's Assyrian wolf on the fold of the Holy Land. But the wariness quickly fuses with something else: astonishment, incredulity.

We sit scattered among the visitors drinking coffee and tea at small wrought-iron tables. They are low key, not intrusive. Not one of them mumbles the litany that has become *de rigeur* at first contact between Jews and nice Germans of middle age . . . "The awful things that happened then . . . *ganz unglaublich* . . . unbelievable how Hitler and his henchmen could have done this and kept it from the *Volk* . . . my parents were shocked when their Jewish friends suddenly disappeared to God knows where. . . ." At such moments my fists clench, I want to hit out but don't, and before turning on my heels I ask how come they didn't know, hadn't read the *Stürmer*, the *Schwarze Korps*, hadn't heard Himmler or Goebbels or Streicher on the Jewish Question, saw no letters from the Eastern Front in which so-ordinary Wehrmacht soldiers described some of the experience. *"Wir Fahren nach Polen um Juden zu Versolen"*—To the East We Ride, to Pickle the Jews' Hide—declaimed the streamers on the trains that took smiling conscripts to the East. "No, of course not, I can swear to that . . . the conspiracy of silence . . . we weren't told. . . ." There are variations on the theme. A bright young Viennese woman at a dinner party back in my Berkeley days referred in one and the same breath to the regrettable things she suspected had happened in the "prison institutions" for Jews and to her own dreadful experiences when the Russians entered the city; on these she elaborated at length. She was a little girl then, the troops were crude and scary, real barbarians, there was so little to eat, for weeks her family had to lug heavy sacks of potatoes from abandoned farmyards, everything around in ruins, she had heard of a friend who was violated, months went by before there was a return to a tolerable life. She had tears in her eyes as she remembered the potatoes.

Tonight, at the Holyland, there is none of that. No equalization of the black fortunes of war that befell their people and ours. Neither is there an attempt by the Austrians to ingratiate. No hyperbole. Nor do I perceive the disjunction of roles between pitier and pitied that often breaks up the common ground of understanding with Jews who are sought out by those occasional Germans who deny nothing and would whitewash nothing. Rather, the plane of interaction this evening is even, uninterrupted. The warmth coming from these people bears no semblance of the patina of offhand *Gemütlichkeit* that is their cultural artifact and that conveys nothing of the person. These Ichthys people do convey something. They convey, quietly, ingenuously, a sharing of pain. Helmuth had already articulated this sense in his talks with me. Their God was crucified for mankind's sins, and in this century their nation has once more committed deicide in the murder of God's people; they bear that cross. Tonight that is not verbalized, only the sense of it is palpable in the room. A phrase comes to me: Identification with the transgressed.

After an hour we assemble in the large hall downstairs. Rows of folding chairs, a slightly raised podium, the flag of Israel. Chaim Kol makes introductory comments, and someone from the Israel-Austria friendship society in Tel Aviv. Then Helmuth states their mission. The sincerity is infectious. We Israelis glance at each other, acknowledging that we are taken aback. Even I am, who have heard him before. Then it is our turn. We rise to speak, one at a time, facing a hundred pairs of eyes that reflect the naked candor with which Helmuth made his declaration. I think it is the guilelessness that is confusing, even more than the singlemindedness of the purpose in which they want to involve us. We must rephrase, soften, the words with which we had planned to assert our refusal.

When I hear the others it strikes me anew how easy my family really had it as we made our way out of the trap.

Nearly a third of the Jews of our town didn't make it at all. Until the outbreak of the war, German policy was emigration rather than annihilation. Property was forfeit, of course, but permission could be obtained to leave with a few suitcases of personal belongings. That was granted only after baroque obstructions. One of the more treacherous hurdles was the requirement of a certificate of unblemished good citizenship from the local police; that opened doors to possibilities. A large donation of cash or jewelry to the *Winterhilfe* or another Nazi fund was helpful proof. Before Gestapo cadres from Germany took over, the resident Austrian officers could be easygoing and even helpful to Jews they knew personally and against whom the population bore no particular animus, *"die weissen Juden"*—the white Jews. In the early months after the Anschluss, some were even allowed to ship ahead crates of furniture and household belongings.

Prior to the *Kristallnacht* in November, the Austrian Jews who were

taken to Dachau and other concentration camps in Germany were largely those who stood out, members of political parties that had opposed
the Nazis, journalists and intellectuals who had taken a public anti-Nazi
stand, people against whom, after a falling out, someone held an account that now could be squared. The camps then were not yet massive
killing institutions; they were, rather, known as the playgrounds of the
S.A. where brown-shirted storm troopers could let sadistic imagination
run wild. Prisoners were brutally abused, many were tortured, and some
were killed; but many could still be bought out provided certain under-
standings were reached. Herr Schotten and Herr Reininger and several
other men were carried off to Dachau the first nights after the Germans
entered. They were released months later on condition of immediate
rearrest and execution should they be found on German territory after
seven days. The Schottens slipped across the Italian border, they survived in an internment camp and, when that fell under German control
in 1944, they hid with partisans. The Reiningers managed within the
week of grace to trade a considerable fortune of family heirlooms for a
Uruguayan passport, went into hiding in Vienna, and eventually stole
their way across borders and to a harbor, where they embarked for
South America.

Illegal crossings, for most of us. The refugee as pariah. That was it,
the trap was doubly sprung. Police and Gestapo acquiescence was not
enough. There had to be a visa of entry to a country of refuge. That
required, first of all, an affidavit of financial responsibility for the would-
be immigrant from citizens of that country. And there had to be transit
visas to a foreign port from which to go on. Jews stood in endless lines,
lines that doubled back on themselves for blocks, in front of American
and other embassies in Vienna and then in Prague and Budapest and
Brussels—wherever the first lap of the journey had landed them—and
waited, affidavits and good conduct certificates and tickets all finally
assembled and clutched tightly in hand, for the audience with a consul
who could, if he wished, write out the ultimate piece of paper that was
the key to survival. But so often he didn't wish, not all that fast, certainly. And the Jews waited. Waited for days and weeks and months. Scattered among them in the serpentine line there also stood a few gentiles,
peasants and artisans and workmen. The consular officials several times
daily walked along the line, scanning. They knew who was who. The
farmers and laborers were culled out, taken in, and shortly emerged set

on their way to a new life. It was called preferred treatment for desirable immigrants.

Not so much later, the Germans devised another form of special treatment for those left standing in the lines, when the generosity of solving Europe's Jewish Problem by enforced departure ended at locked gates of entry. For the meantime, the Viennese S.A. and *Hitler Jugend* every so often lent a hand in shortening the lines by beating up waiting men whose particularly offensive Jewish physiognomies were intolerable in the newly gentrified streets. A few countries granted asylum to transports of small numbers of children. Some people succeeded in going down the Danube to the Black Sea in an assortment of makeshift craft, anything that hopefully could float, and from there continued in derelict cargo steamers to the coast of Palestine. The *Paritas*. The *Struma*. A flotilla of smaller vessels. The passage in the crammed, listing hulks was nightmarish. Some of them sank in the Danube, the Black Sea, and the Mediterranean, with most of those on board. Some reached the shores only to find them sealed. The Balfour Declaration had mandated Palestine as a Jewish Homeland but the British felt obliged to placate the growing Arab nationalist movements. Haj Amin El-Husseini, the mufti of Jerusalem, later reciprocated by recruiting a division of Bosnian Muslims for Hitler's S.S. The British didn't care that much for Jewish refugees in any event; that was voiced plaintively by Minister of State for the Middle East Lord Moyne, contemplating late in the war the prospect of an influx of displaced persons who might survive the German killing institutions, "What am I to do with all those Jews?" The British issued their White Paper in 1939: Jewish entry was restricted to a trickle. The *Struma* was turned back in 1942 by Turkish authorities in compliance with British orders; nearly eight hundred refugees who had come aboard in Rumania were lost when the boat foundered in the Black Sea. Some of the boats evaded the blockade, before and during the war and after the defeat of the Axis Powers. Many did not, and their passengers were taken off, often forcibly, and held in detention camps until they could be shipped out to other camps in Mauritius and Cyprus.

Now Tirzah is speaking. A small, white-haired woman, still attractive in her early seventies, she served in the *Palmach*, the strike force of the *Haganah* which held down British troops in diversionary engagements so that the illegal refugees could make it ashore through the surf from craft that had eluded British surveillance. She acquired a reputation for both courage and charm. She has a slight speech impediment in her later years, but she tells the story of her arrival in Palestine clearly and dispassionately.

She was on one of three unseaworthy freighters that left a Romanian port in September 1940 with several thousand Jews who were bound, illegally, for Palestine, including the last shipment of refugees from Austria that the Nazi authorities allowed to leave. The freighters made it through the Black Sea and sailed on into the Mediterranean. Constantly dodging the British blockade, they changed course repeatedly. When interception seemed imminent, they steamed back to international waters where maritime law guaranteed immunity from seizure. The British patrol ships ignored the ordinance. After a journey of two months, the ships were intercepted at sea, forced toward the coast and escorted to anchor in the outer harbor of Haifa. Leaders of Palestine's Jewish community pleaded with the government in London for suspension of the ban on immigration for the starved and exhausted men, women, and children. The plea was rejected. While the refugees were being transferred to a chartered liner, the *Patria,* for deportation, a *Haganah* squad placed an explosive charge inside the *Patria*'s hull, below the waterline. The damage was intended to cause the boat to scuttle slowly, with ample time to evacuate its human cargo. The British subscribed to another maritime charter, that persons shipwrecked off a shore were entitled to shelter in that land and could not forcibly be expelled to another. The *Haganah* thought the British might observe that one. But the calculations went wrong. The *Patria*'s fabric was too rotten. The blast, on November 25th, blew out a large section of its side, and the boat keeled over and capsized within minutes; 260 people perished. Tirzah managed to scramble from the submerging deck down the side, now horizontal in the waves, and held on to a hawser until she was pulled off and taken to the beach. Among the victims were some of her relatives. The survivors were permitted to stay. The 1,600 remaining refugees were held for a few days in a stockade in Atlith, and transported on another boat to Mauritius. A large number succumbed there to disease and deprivation during the four-and-a-half years of detainment.

"So you see, it wasn't an easy homecoming!" Tirzah continues, running her eyes across the faces which are turned to her in fixed absorption. Leo Blum, she tells us, the man whose nephew served in the Golani Brigade with my oldest son, was also on the *Patria* with his parents and sister. He will tell the same story when the Ichthys people meet with ours in the Galilee. Tirzah goes on for a few minutes more, describing her youth in Wr. Neustadt and then her life in Israel, the hard early years after she was let in, the smoother ones thereafter. And then she begins the explanation all of us had already framed, individually and in conversation with each other, why she, why we, can't bring ourselves to return. Helmuth has already said it unequivocally, that no matter how deeply important it is for him and the Ichthys church that we come, our reluctance will be understood with compassion and respect. Tirzah pauses. She looks again, hard, at the upturned faces. Some have tears in their eyes. Tirzah falters. She cries. Then she says very rapidly, the emotion now undisguised, the words not quite distinct, tripping over each other: "I said I can't come . . . but look . . . I've grown old . . . I've become soft. I am looking at you . . . I am not sure of myself now. . . ." A long pause. "I've broken down." She cries and then she laughs. "I can't say 'No' to you. I am coming."

The others speak. Other stories. Nothing I have not heard and read before from survivors, nothing unusual in these Jewish sagas of the mid-twentieth century, but as I listen to the stories recited now in this stilled room to a group of Austrian Christians who want to shoulder something of the anguish, as I listen to them from the people with whom I grew up, the hurt and the sorrow take on a searing immediacy. Many lost their parents in the death camps and in British detention in the tropics. Some lived through German and British camps themselves. Some landed on the coast of Palestine under British fire, were rescued by the *Haganah*, and passed from one kibbutz and urban hiding place to another. A few were on the *Exodus* that reached Haifa with 4,500 displaced persons in July of 1947. The *Exodus* was boarded by British marines; the refugees resisted and suffered casualties before being returned to German soil.

When they finally could begin taking root in Palestine, several of the Wr. Neustädters enlisted in the Jewish Brigade and under British flag fought the greater enemy in Italy; others fought the Arab irregular bands that raided the Jewish settlements and, after Israel came into being as an independent state, against the invading armies of the Arab countries. There were years of hardship for them all, years of malaria and insecurity in the fledgling kibbutzim in which many made their homes.

Of all those at the Holyland that evening, my journey to safety was indeed the least precarious. When it is my turn to speak, I am almost ashamed to tell my story in this company. There is too much of a contrast. As I come to the moment of decision, I too find myself defenseless, disarmed by my old childhood friends and, yes, by these strange new Austrian ones, the resolve is gone, and I repeat Tirzah's words: "Perhaps I have become soft. I no longer can say 'No.' I am also coming." And that is how each one of us concludes. We have each come full circle these past hours.

The meeting with the Eiwens' group up in the Galilee ends identically. The same turnabout, even by those who were most unambiguous in their conviction to have nothing to do with these people and their proposal beyond a polite one-time gathering, on our home ground. When we talk with each other later we share the bewilderment of our reactions. How come? What got to us, made us change course?

When the Eiwens write to the Wr. Neustädters in the States, South America, England, and Wales, the response is mixed. Only a few accept, and that after hearing of the sudden change of mind of the Israelis. Several write back, politely declining on the same grounds as I had, as we all had, until we came face to face with Helmuth and Uli. A few do not answer at all; that option leapt to my mind when Chaim Kol first called to ask if I would be willing to meet this pastor. It seems that passion and intensity expressed in words alone sometimes fall short; the confrontations with Ichthys in Jerusalem and in the Galilee were informed by something that we had not foreseen and that we could not quite convey to each other with words afterwards.

The *Woche der Begegnung* will take place in May.

David W. Weiss's father, Heinrich Hillel Weiss, as a captain in
the Honved Hussar regiment of the Austro-Hungarian army,
1916–1917.

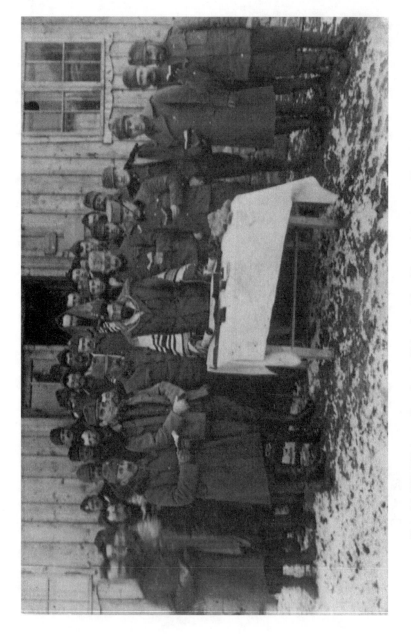

Heinrich Hillel Weiss reading the *megillah* to Jewish soldiers of the Austro-Hungarian army on Purim, at the Russian front, 1917.

Rabbi Heinrich Hillel Weiss, New York, ca. 1950.

David Weiss's mother, Julie (Yula) Kohn, age 17,
Vienna, 1917.

Julie Kohn, Vienna, early 1920s.

The artist David Kohn, David Weiss's maternal grandfather, in his studio in Vienna before World War I.

David Kohn with students in his art academy in Vienna before World War I.

Red crayon portrait of Kaiser Franz Josef I, done by David Kohn in
Schönbrunn Palace, Vienna, 1915.

Aranka Flesch (born Friedenthal), David Weiss's cousin, and her daughter, Erika, Sarvar, Hungary, 1936. Mother and daughter were killed in Auschwitz in 1944.

Mina Gneist, the Weisses' housekeeper, with Friede Weiss, age 2,
and David Weiss, age 5, Wiener Neustadt, 1932.

Mina Gneist with husband Hans, Wiener Neustadt, 1938.

Fourth-grade class picture, Übungsschule, with head teacher Herr Leposchitz, Wiener Neustadt, 1937. David Weiss is in the middle row, fifth from left.

Temple in Wiener Neustadt, late 1920s, photograph from city archives.

Temple in Wiener Neustadt, desecrated by S.A. stormtroopers, the morning
after Kristallnacht, November 10, 1938.

Hauptplatz (central square) in Wiener Neustadt, 1950s, postcard.

Number 11 on the Hauptplatz, 1979. The Weiss family lived on the
top floor in the 1920s and 1930s.

A THOUSAND YEARS IN A
BLOOD-STAINED LAND

J ews are known to have lived in Austria as early as the tenth century. They arrived in larger numbers at the beginning of the thirteenth, fleeing from widespread persecutions in the Rhineland and Bavaria. There is a record of a prayer house in Vienna in 1204, and within a few years Jews were settling in several Austrian towns— Klosterneuburg, Tulln, Krems, and Wr. Neustadt. The Jewish community expanded in the next decades and became home to scholars whose works can still be found today on bookshelves of Judaic libraries. By 1230 Jews were playing an appreciable role in the country's commerce. But over the succeeding centuries waves of oppression and exile periodically imperiled their existence. The pattern was recurrent. The Church was unremittingly hostile to this people that it had demonized and that remained stubbornly loyal to the faith of its fathers, an intransigently, visibly alien element in Christian towns and villages. They were hounded through the years not only for the archetypal crimes of rejecting the divinity of the Galilean preacher and contriving his crucifixion but also for the persistent repetition of the act of deicide: They were accused of putting their hands when they could on the consecrated wafer of the Eucharist and piercing it till it bled. In recent years a less diabolic theory has been advanced for the reddish exudate that sometimes appeared on the sacred bread; the metabolic activity of a ubiquitous bacterium, *Serratia marcescens*. And in a macabre inversion of the Church's paramount rite, the Jews were charged with using the blood of sacrificed Christian children for preparation of the unleavened Pass-over bread. European churches have shrines to these canonized child martyrs.

The populace responded to the incitement by priests and prelates with holy fury. The plagues and famines and disasters of war that punc-tuated European history were readily attributed to the wrath of God brought on by the sufferance of this blasphemous people in their midst. The intractable alienness of the Jews was cause enough for dislike and suspicion, and their presence provided specific explanations for calam-ity: A people given to God's assassination was surely not above venge-fully poisoning the wells from which His redeemed believers drew water. Some of the more worldly kings and dukes may quietly have doubted the theological and xenophobic underpinnings of Jew-hatred. They had been known to oppose the Church in other matters. But they had compelling reasons of their own. Expropriations of the property of the Jews added to dwindling state coffers and expulsion canceled debts to Jews who, barred from more honorable professions, were forced into moneylending as a means of subsistence.

The collusion between secular and Church authorities was cata-strophic. Following an accusation of ritual murder or the host's desecra-tion, whole communities were incarcerated and their leaders tortured. Expulsions from towns, from regions, from country. Forced conversions. Many Jews chose death over baptism. In 1420, two hundred and seventy who refused the sacrament were burned at the stake in Vienna. The country came to be known as *eretz ha-damim*, the blood-stained land.

The episodes of violence and banishment were repetitive. Inter-spersed in the annals of Austria's Jews there were occasional periods of greater toleration. During one such interval, from 1440 to 1490, they were again permitted to settle in the Steiermark and Kärnten, and a center of Jewish learning sprang up in Wr. Neustadt. These times of sufferance were usually prompted by economic exigency. Compelled to perennial migration over the continent, linked closely to each oth-er across borders by ties of family and shared identity, and mandated to trade and monetary dealings, the Jews acquired a reputation for fi-nancial acumen. Their banishment was often followed by the country's economic decline and they were called back when the need for mer-cantile and monetary rejuvenation became pressing. They would return on assurances of certain privileges and for the more common pressing reason that, harried as they were from place to place, perpetual wanderers, no offer of accommodation, no matter how tenuous it may have seemed, could be ignored. And tenuous the invitations proved to be for those who returned. They paid a heavy Jews' tax, in gold. Their daily lives were overseen and tightly regulated. Approval had to be gained for a change of residence, for marriage, for the number of children allowed a family, even for the curricula of the *yeshivoth*. And again and again, once the economy improved, the Church would lead monarch or prince to another cycle of dispossession and eviction.

Only at the close of the eighteenth century, under the liberal rule of Kaiser Josef II, did a process of equalization begin for the Empire's Jews. The punitive tax and the obligation to wear the yellow patch were lifted, freedom of occupation was granted, and the doors to schools and universities were opened. The French Revolution and abolition of the ghetto in the wake of Napoleon's conquests accelerated progress toward liberation and equality in Western Europe. In 1848, Austria's parliament granted the Jews civil rights. The Jewish population increased rapidly. Flourishing communities came to life throughout the country. By 1910, one hundred seventy-five thousand Jews resided in Vienna, and by 1938 their number had neared 200,000.

Yet the history of Austria's Jews had not mellowed into a golden age of acceptance. The road to civil liberty was not straightforward; there were bleak interims of standstill and bleaker ones of reversal. Anti-Semitism, deeply rooted in the populace in its germinal Christ-killer guise, was reinforced in the latter nineteenth century by an amalgam of darkly romantic Germanic ethnocentricity and the emerging pseudo-science of racial purity and eugenics. The turn-of-the-century mayor of Vienna, Karl Lueger, attempted to turn back the clock on Jewish rights, but could not overcome the resistance of another Kaiser disposed to tolerance, Franz Josef I. Lueger left as a legacy his publicly declaimed yearning for the day when the trees lining the city's promenades would be decorated with hanging Jews.

We old Austrian Jews cherished our slowly won equality before the law, and we continued to exist before the unwavering animus of very many of our countrymen. Until 1938, when that animus sprang out into the light of day, like a demon held captive too long in a loosely stoppered magic jar.

The Burgenland is the eastern province of Austria, stretching along the border with Hungary. Its name derives from the many castles set on the hills that dot the fertile farmland. Jews were living in the area as early as the fourteenth century but, as elsewhere, their sojourn was intermittently interrupted by waves of dislodgment. It was not until many years later that their community began to thrive and, eventually, to take on a character of its own. In the 1670s, after the Jewish population of Austria proper was cast out once again, a few refugees from Bohemia and Moravia moved into the Burgenland. Then, in 1690, the ruler of the province, Count Esterházy, issued a remarkable declaration. The Jews were granted communal autonomy and protection from attack; in times of disorder or war they were to find safety in the strongholds of the domain. Although, as usual, a heavy tax was extracted for the privilege of establishing roots in the land, the degree of security that was promised was unusual. Groups of Jews were drawn to the area during the next century and a half, including several eminent families from Vienna.

The small towns in which they first congregated—Eisenstadt, Mattersburg, Lackenbach, Kobersdorf, Deutschkreuz, Kittsee, and Frauenkirchen—came to be known in Jewish life as the Seven Communities. Functioning in close cooperation with each other, they achieved a singular civic and cultural commonality. Far less affected by the currents of assimilation that swept Western and Central European Jewry as political emancipation progressed through the nineteenth century, the Burgenland Jews remained, for the most, deeply committed to traditional Judaism. Their rabbis and *yeshivoth* set standards of scholarship and piety. A distinctive pattern of religious observance and custom took shape among them, and although the Jewish population at its height did not reach much above 4,500, the Burgenland became a mainstay of Orthodoxy in the lands of the Austro-Hungarian monarchy. Many of the region's Jews were engaged as manual workers and craftsmen, others worked in the more commonplace occupations of Jews, as shopkeepers, small merchants, and traveling salesmen. Families were large, and family enterprises and homesteads could usually absorb no more than one or two of the older adult sons. As younger children reached maturity they founded smaller satellite communities in neighboring villages. Jewish venders and peddlers visited the weekly markets and seasonal fairs of Wr. Neustadt, the largest nearby town, but it was not until the latter part of the century that Jews were given leave to stay overnight. When after World War I Wr. Neustadt grew into a significant industrial as well as mercantile center that offered better opportunities for a livelihood, Jews from the Burgenland settled there and formed the nucleus—and much of the character—of what became the country's second largest Jewish community.

There was an intermittent Jewish presence in Wr. Neustadt from soon after the town received its charter as a *Statutarstadt* in 1192. In the fifteenth century, in the decades when a vigorous community could establish itself, its members contributed not only to the town's economy but also to its defense against attack. "Their spiritual leaders would permit them to do all manner of work on the Sabbath to protect the city from its enemies, in accordance with the instructions of the gentile citizens and noblemen," wrote one of its rabbis. In 1496, they were nonetheless expelled. In the early years of the eighteenth century, refugees from Ödenburg, across the border with Hungary, once more ventured a Jewish return to Wr. Neustadt; they were shortly driven out again under clerical agitation. The first Jew in modern times to be allowed residence, in 1848, was a man named Friedenthal, one of whose descendants, a rabbi, married my aunt Paula from Pressburg. It was only in 1870 that a Jewish community was officially constituted in Wr. Neustadt, and not until 1889 that it was privileged to open a cemetery. A synagogue in Moorish style—*der Tempel*—was built in 1902. Twenty years later Heinrich Hillel Weiss was appointed its rabbi, and set for his congregation the tone of an enlightened orthodox Judaism that was fully engaged with the knowledge and the affairs of the world at large. The Jewish population of the town stood at well over a thousand in 1938, not counting persons of Jewish background who had converted or who no longer identified themselves as adherents of the Mosaic religion; those, too, fell under the ban of the Nüremberg racial laws and shared the fate of the congregation when Austria chose to become the eastern province—the Ostmark—of the Third Reich.

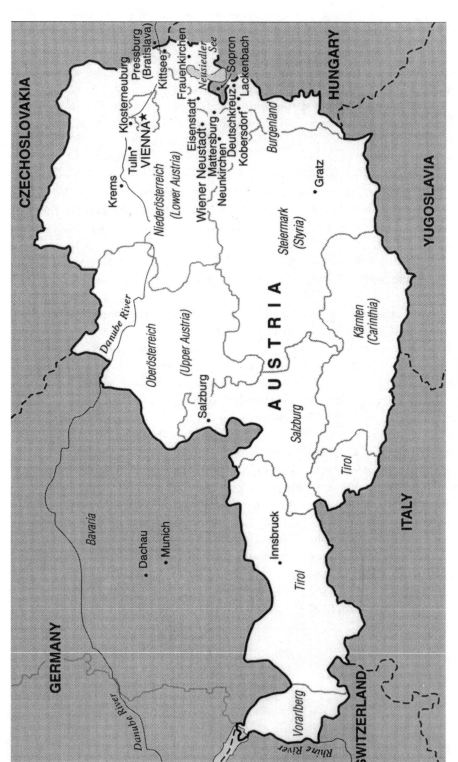

Austria, 1938

Chapter 10

WIENER NEUSTADT, MARCH 1938, AND ESCAPE

MARCH 11, 1938, WR. NEUSTADT, LATE AFTERNOON

A middle-aged couple stood in the hallway of our apartment on the Hauptplatz. Refugees from Germany, they had joined Wr. Neustadt's congregation a few years earlier and become close to my parents. They wouldn't sit, they were in great haste. Two small suitcases stood at the entrance. Several large bills of foreign currency and an envelope were held out to my father. They were pleading.

"Herr Oberrabbiner, please, we beg you . . . leave everything, now . . . at once. There isn't a moment to lose. Throw some clothing into a bag and come with us. We have money for you, and tickets on the flight to Prague. The Germans will be here by morning. It's your last chance to get out. Now, please, don't wait!"

"But that's impossible," my father replied. "I can't leave everything just like that! The people . . . the *Tempel* . . . and everything we have. And there really is no need to run! You'll see! Schuschnigg won't let them in without a fight, and the Germans aren't ready for war . . . that would bring Mussolini into it. The Italians won't tolerate German troops on their border! Surely not! Mussolini has said that. And there is the plebiscite next week. You'll see! The Social Democrats and the Catholics won't vote for Hitler, he is against them, too. I understand you," my father added, "you've gone through it in Germany, but Austria is different."

They cried, hugged my parents, and left.

That night Schuschnigg abdicated. He bade farewell to Austria, he would spare his country bloodshed, there was to be no resistance, and the Germans had promised to honor the people's will in the plebiscite.

We woke in the morning to a town transformed. A malignant transformation.

Every public building was draped with huge streamers of the Third Reich's colors, the ancient mystic motif of the swastika, inverted, black, in a white circle centered on a field of blood-red. The same banners waved from flag poles, from windows and roofs of private houses, from stores, over the sides of cars and lorries. The streets and squares were teeming. Some German soldiers. Many more townspeople. It seemed as if everyone who could walk or stand was out. Men, women, even young children with swastika pins of bronze or silver in the lapels of jacket and blouse. Large numbers of the ordinary men of Wr. Neustadt in the brown uniform and jackboots of the S.A., the *Sturmabteilung*, the Nazi Party's storm troopers. The Horst Wessel Lied blaring from radios, groups of people on the corners joining in, the crowds carried along and away by the mesmerizing beat and cadenced stanzas of the S.A.'s anthem, *"Die Strasse frei, den braunen Batallionen, die Strasse frei, dem Sturm-Abteilungs-Mann . . ."* —make way, the brown battalions march, the storm-troop man has right of way . . . —that reach a crescendo in a bellowed utopian coda, *"Wenn Judenblut vom Messer spritzt, dann wird alles gut sein . . ."* —when Jewish blood shall spurt from knife, all shall be well with us. . . . The town was seized with delirious jubilation. When I think about it now, there come to mind Thomas Bernhard's astringent images of the paroxysm of elation that shuddered through the vast throng assembled in the Heldenplatz to welcome Adolf Hitler to Vienna.

Where did all the hard signs and symbols and men of the New Order spring from, so suddenly, overnight, we wondered as we looked down from between the slats of our living room's lowered wooden blinds. It was perhaps a naive wondering. I remember our last summer's vacation before the Anschluss in a Jewish-owned boardinghouse in Seefeld, in the Tyrol. One day as I retrieved a ball from the undergrowth that bordered the basement lodging of the caretaker, a man who was outgoing and friendly with the guests and their children, I glanced up into his room and saw the entire ceiling painted with the Nazi flag. I mentioned nothing to my parents. Had the auguries been there, prevalent, all along, and we Jews had chosen to make light of them until they were thrust into our faces with fury?

Our introduction to what it meant to be Jewish in the transformed town and country came at once, together with the euphoria that transported our fellow citizens. We were, in fact, no longer citizens. It took some weeks and months for that fact to become enshrined in the Ostmark's law. With a quite exceptional alacrity, legislative measure upon measure were enacted. We were progressively stripped of Austrian nationality and of our civil rights. Jewish stores and property were placed under "Aryan" management and, shortly thereafter, ownership. Bank accounts and insurance policies were frozen, to remain unthawed. Jews were dismissed from their positions in the universities, the civil service, from any public employment. The population was warned against having recourse to Jewish physicians and lawyers, who would take every opportunity to debauch Aryan women and defraud Aryan clients. The people's boycott of Jewish concerns and Jewish professionals was to be sweeping, an expression of the too-long slumbering but now awakened pride of the German masses. To make certain of the spontaneity of the Volk's reborn will and determination, Jewish perfidy and villainy were meticulously depicted with mounting tempo and ferocity in the pages of newspapers and children's books, taught in the schoolroom, pronounced from officeholder's rostrum and from the pulpits of churches.

That we had become the lepers of society was brought home to us before and without benefit of due process. The afternoon of the first day, my parents sent me to buy fish at Czerny's, where we had been customers for many years; it would be safer for a child to venture out into this new uncertain world. I didn't enter the store. A large sign in the shop window, black lettered, informed the public that dogs and Jews were unwanted. Similar announcements were everywhere, on gentile stores, cafes, restaurants. The park benches carried their version: NICHT FÜR JUDEN—Not for Jews.

The following night, a member of my father's congregation died. He was an iron dealer in Neunkirchen. His scrap-metal yard was guarded by four enormous Great Danes. My father used to tell me that visiting

Mundl was something of an adventure, the dogs rearing up and plac-
ing their front paws on his shoulders until Mundl got them down.
That night, they were of no help to him. When men entered the premises, the dogs didn't even bark. Mundl was taken away, and was found
hanging in a police cell next morning. I knew the balding, easygoing
man who had always seemed an accepted fixture of the village scene.
When inquiries were made of the police, the family was informed that
"the Jew" had been brought in by some patriotic Austrians for reasons
unknown and had some hours later committed suicide. No further questions would be considered. That was my first experience of real terror. If
Mundl, so much the old-time Austrian, so very much like the workers
and peasants among whom he and his forebears had lived, could so
simply, so casually, vanish into death, why not, too, my father, who did
look different in his rabbinic beard and black coat?

The terrible fear of that was reinforced in the coming weeks. A number of men were taken from their homes at night by squads of S.A. and
police and sent to Dachau. Among them were the president and other
officers of the congregation. No word of their fate came back for months.
We only knew that Dachau was a place of horror. Would my father's
turn come this night or the next?

He was brave. The frightened community turned to him, and he
found the strength to give encouragement. "The worst will be over soon,
you'll see!" I heard him say again and again. "They are human beings,
too, and there must be intelligent ones among their leaders. Once the
Pöbel—the riffraff—get it out of their system, saner heads will prevail.
This is the twentieth century, we mustn't forget! We'll have to ride it out
for a while and when things simmer down we'll find a way to manage."
My mother would add her touch of humanism to the analysis, "We
mustn't generalize. Not every Nazi is a Jew-hater. I am sure of that.
There are other reasons why some of them joined the Party. The depression . . . the unemployment . . . one must understand." Some time later,
when sympathetic Nazis failed to appear on the scene, she somewhat
narrowed her perspective: Nazis were indeed just that, Nazis, benight-
ed anti-Semites, but there were many decent Germans and Austrians,
too. She was firm in that differentiation. The only time I can remember
being struck in the face by her was when I exclaimed one day, "Die
verfluchten Deutschen"—the damned Germans. Slap. "You are not to say
that again! You can say 'damned Nazis' but not 'damned Germans.'

There are many good people among them, too." She was a great admirer of Goethe and Schiller and Rilke.

Their posture of confidence was transparent. The fear that gripped my father as it did all of us could not be entirely disguised. His beard had been coal-black. By June it had turned nearly white. Whenever the door bell rang, he flinched. That remained with him even after we fled, until he died in 1954, in New York. And my fear for him remained with me as long as he lived, shaking me in recurrent nightmares of cowering in bed as men in brown lead him away. I think that it has continued with me to the present, transposed to a relentless anxiety for the safety of my sons and their children.

And yet, even as our expulsion from normal life proceeded, step by step, edict by edict, we tried to resist reality. Especially those of Wr. Neustadt's community whose roots went far back in Austria's history. We could not bring ourselves to see that the handwriting on the wall was not merely the graffiti of vandals but rather a nation's declaration of intent. The children of the men in Dachau wrote a letter to Adolf Hitler. I helped with the composition. Surely, we pleaded, he, the leader of Germany, could not be aware of what was being done in his name; the men who were taken away were, every one of them, upright, law-abiding citizens; they were loyal Austrians, had served with distinction on the front; please, respected Führer, look into the matter and instruct your officers to bring them home again.

My parents fared better than many of the town's Jews. My father's stature, the respect accorded him in the old days, held for a while. And my mother had achieved a reputation of her own. She was a peculiar fusion of ideals. Deeply religious—if she questioned her faith in orthodox Judaism, I was not aware of it, not as a child, not in adulthood—she also held to a firm conviction that communism would accomplish for the world the Torah's ethos of social justice. She hated poverty and injustice. That hatred was not left abstract. Walking with me in the streets during the depression years of the early 1930s when Wr. Neustadt's industries shut down, she would be outraged at the sight of a ragged, hungry-looking urchin. Hunger was, so she instructed me, an abomination in the sight of God and man, and abomination it was whether it stared from a Jewish face or a gentile face. Want was commonplace those years among the families of the factory workers. We were not wealthy, but my father had a salary, and there was money for food and clothing. My mother would grab the passing child by the arm, walk him into the nearest grocery and buy half a loaf of bread, slices of ham, a bag of cookies. Sometimes it was a pair of shoes, sometimes a shirt. Friday was beggar's day, when the very poor were permitted to go about the town freely seeking alms, with no harassment from the police. They would arrive late morning at the rabbi's door, sometimes as many as fifteen and even more, after they had been to the parsonage. There they had received the standard allocation, a few *Groschen*, enough for a small chunk of bread. They did better at our place; that was common knowledge. My mother had baked many loaves of *challah*, boiled several dozen eggs, and a large pot of the soup that we would have at the Sabbath table that night stood ready for the morning guests, kept warm on the vestibule's *Kachelofen*, next to stacks of bowls and spoons. Always the pedagogue—she was an ardent follower of Montessori, wrote articles for an educational magazine, *Mutter und Kind*—I would be given a brief lecture just before the poor were given their meal: "The Talmud says that enjoying a good meal while there are hungry people next door is an offense to God."

The accuracy of her Jewish citations was questionable, I sensed even then; like most women of her time, she had received only a minimum of religious instruction. When she decided to study medicine, she ran head-on into the categorical objections of her father the *Hofmaler*: Mixing with the "free" university student crowd was a risk he would not condone for his only daughter. She had remonstrated, she told me when I was older, that he himself was an artist—was the crowd among whom he studied in the art academies any more inclined toward piety? His was a faith that could not be shaken, he had replied, not quite to the point, and that was that. She was an independent, obstinate woman and she had not accepted lightly her disbarment from a career in medicine. But with that option closed, she threw herself, with all her formidable energy and intelligence, into other ways of improving the lot of humanity. She made her stern parent's reflex to charity her own. Later, in America, she became a nurse's aide, and gave much of her days to caring for the aged, destitute people of my father's Yiddish-speaking immigrant congregation on New York's Lower East Side. Many of them were helpless in their tenement flats after surgery for advanced malignant disease. Those years persuaded her that cancer, perhaps even more than poverty, was mankind's foremost affliction, and that I, her one son, named after the *Hofmaler,* must learn to focus my quantum of the generational reflex accordingly. I also have a good measure of rebelliousness in my makeup, inherited or acquired, and I resolved firmly to find my own way, not to fit into a script programmed by others. *Sic transit gloria mundi.* I wound up directing an institute of cancer research, and in spare hours I write articles on Jewish theology.

Back then, in Wr. Neustadt, my mother fed the poor and I was her assistant. I organized a group of Jewish children who collected money for packages of groceries to be distributed to the indigent before holy days. Throughout my grade school years, I brought to class a lunch package for two. Two pumpernickel sandwiches, the filling of goose schmalz, two apples. One for me, one for the Haslinger boy, a Catholic; his father was a carpenter who had done some work in our apartment and who had lost his livelihood when the furniture factory folded.

My mother taught and educated anyone who would give her a hearing. Her husband's congregants, on the rights of women that are guaranteed in Jewish law but whose expression is often hindered by the mores and prejudices of male society. Teachers and school officials, on the rights and sensibilities of children. And a predominant endeavor was the education of Mina Gneist.

Hermine Gneist. I cannot recall her maiden name. She had been part of the family from before I was born, and for me she was simply Mina, just as my mother was Mutti and I would have to think for a moment when asked by someone for her name . . . Yula, Julie.

Girls of peasant stock often entered service in Austrian middle-class households when still in their teens, to assist the lady of the house at whatever needed doing. Usually, the young women remained servants, working fixed hours at specified tasks—maid, cook, laundress, mother's helper. But sometimes the association grew into intimacy; the employee entered the circle of the family. Mina lived with us, as one of us. She visited her own family infrequently. She worked with my mother, rather than for her. My mother could not accede to a vertical relationship with someone in her home. She made Mina her colleague and confidante. My father regarded her as something of a distant cousin who had come to stay. Were I to record the dynamics of my daily childhood existence geometrically, I would draw myself within a field of vectors running two-directionally between the focal points of comfort and authority,

Mina and Mutti, my very busy father's line intermittently appearing and fading across the diagram.

Mina was raised a Catholic, but her gospel of redemption she drew from my mother's creed of social justice. My mother was a relentless catechist; Mina who came to us before she was seventeen, an apt novitiate. Blonde, blue-eyed, attractive, very sure of her powers, I see her in my mind's eye stopping on walks with me and my younger sister in the Akademie, the national military academy whose wooded grounds were open to the public, taunting the smart cadets: "You, with your spit and polish! Just wait, the Russians are coming. Then we'll all have our daily bread. We won't need guns and uniforms any more. There will be democracy! You'll tuck in your tails and run home to mom. Hah!" The soldiers tried bantering back, but they were intimidated by the outbursts. Mina kept that up even after the Germans arrived, chivvying the S.A. men and German troops, until my frightened parents stopped her. Mina, it seemed, was frightened of no one when she was incensed. Her contempt for Nazis was vehement. *"Braunes Gesindel!"*—brown trash— she would mutter audibly as S.A. marched by.

She married Hans Gneist. I was a member of the engagement. Hans, a painter, had come to whitewash rooms in the apartment. We struck up a friendship. I was enchanted when he made me a menagerie of farm animals from putty and clay, and I didn't want him to leave when the job was done. Rather, I proposed to him and Mina that they could marry, and then he would be around to play with me. She was embarrassed and laughed. When I persisted, Mina told me to shut up. He was nice enough, she admitted, but she would accept his invitation for an evening out only after they had a "serious talk" together. I had an idea of what that talk would partly be about; I advised Hansi to call on her with a bouquet of cornflowers, a symbol of the socialists. No problem there, Hans offered, his views tended in that direction anyway. They were wed a year later. Mina moved in with him but continued to spend her days with us.

Shortly after the Anschluss, Mina organized a group of similar minded "Kindermädchen" and marched on Gestapo headquarters to demand cancellation of the ban on employment by Jews. For the time being, the Gestapo also seemed intimidated. Until the matter could be given a more careful review, no action would be taken against the women to enforce the regulation.

One evening early in April, there was a commotion in the stairwell of our building. Two men in S.S. regalia were lurching up the steep, worn marble steps, shouting epithets. They were going to give the Jews a lesson, they were going to begin with the Jew-rabbi. Where is he? Mina had been sponging floors. She grabbed the bucket of hot, alkaline water, lowered the long-handled mop, and tore open the front door. The men, unsteady on the landing below our apartment, started up. Mina spoke, for her and under the circumstances, rather quietly. The sentences she strung together very fast, before lifting the mop, were in her region's peasant dialect that I barely understood. I gathered that they had to do with ancestries of bastardy and conditions somehow related to maleness that afflicted the S.S. and their Führer. Then she spat: "One more stair, there won't be descendants!" One man dared. The mop swung in a full arc and with an impact that surprised me—Mina was a slight young woman—squarely struck his face. He fell backward, taking the more cautious one along, the two crashing in a heap on the bottom, Mina and her mop after them. I watched from behind the *Kachelofen*. When the men were gone, Mina said: "Don't tell Papa and Mutti! What they don't have to know won't do them harm." They had been in an inner room, not hearing, and Mina surmised correctly: This had been an impromptu call, not an official visit. But what was also clear was that Jews were no longer under the protection of police or court. We were now open game for anyone who did not much care for us, individually or collectively. For my family, Mina had been the protector.

She was that until we left Wr. Neustadt, and later, after my mother's mother was put into a cattle car to Theresienstadt, she kept the old woman alive for three years, until the Russians arrived, with monthly packages of food. Hans was in the Wehrmacht, taken captive by the Americans in Italy. Their two children were sickly, fruit and milk became unattainable as the war went on, and they died. In the last months, Mina smuggled bread to starving Hungarian Jews in the death marches that passed in the snows through the town's suburbs. This time, the S.S. were not intimidated. Mina was arrested and sentenced by a *Volksgericht* to be shot. The Soviet Army took the town before the sentence could be carried out.

We were aided by other gentiles. In the first weeks, when the stores would not sell to Jews, carpenter Haslinger brought food late at night. One of my grade school teachers, Herr Leposchitz, a tall, distinguished gentleman, arrived one afternoon, immaculately dressed, no swastika in lapel, to invite my mother for a stroll. With her turban headdress over the *sheitel*—the wig orthodox married women wear to cover their hair— she was unmistakably a "Jewess," even to the German newcomers who did not know her. Escorting her through the avenues and Stadtpark was an act of courage. There were others who, less demonstratively, let it be known by a gesture or a passing word that they had not lost their regard for this family. Unlike many of the town's Jews, my father was not physically accosted on the streets when we began venturing from our homes after the initial shock of disbelief and fear phased into the routine of legislated displacement and gray uncertainty. I myself was taunted and jostled by Hitler Jugend boys. When the jeering became intolerable one day, after the schools reopened and Jewish pupils briefly returned to class until that loophole in the fabric of exclusion was repaired by law, I for a moment forgot my parents' warning not to hit back—that could lead to my father's detention—and pummeled a bigger kid in his H.J. outfit to the floor. There were no dire consequences.

The plebiscite that was held shortly after the Anschluss was overwhelmingly in favor of Austria's merger into the Third Reich; the percentage of citizens casting the "Ja" was in the high nineties. Even given that the voting was under de facto German occupation and under the Nazi flag, the choice of the great majority was unmistakable. So was the enthusiastic spontaneity with which the fresh canonization of anti-Semitism was welcomed. Often, the spontaneity was ahead of policy. Franz Werfel, in a searing short story, described the popular pogrom that took place the first weeks in the Burgenland. Jews were attacked, beaten, and thrown by the hundreds across the border by a mob of villagers and local storm troopers. The Hungarian border guards turned them back. They were abandoned in a strip of no-man's-land without food or shelter. Women gave birth, infants and older people died.

Although our family was for a time spared much of the extemporaneous harassment, it became obvious that the period of grace could not last. The racial legislation grew increasingly draconian. By late spring, there was talk that Wr. Neustadt was to be made *Judenrein*, cleansed of its Jews, a civic gift to the Führer. The owner of a house we had bought some months earlier filed charges of fraudulence and extortion against my parents. The widow of a ranking officer in the Austrian army, she had been saccharine with me and my sister when we had moved in, providing treats and rides in her Mercedes; now she heeded a boy-friend's counsel, the opportunity should not be missed of recovering both the property and its price. But it was the mockery, ever more often sounded after a passing Jew, that precipitated my father into action. The jingles bespoke a dead end, no extrication. *"Was er glaubt ist einerlei, in der Rasse liegt die Schweinerei"*—what he believes, I could care less, it's in the race, the swinishness; and *"Judas verrecke im eigenen Drecke"*—Judas, expire, in your excrement's mire. Favored status would not for-ever shield us from the curse of Judas in our genes; and, long before genes and genotype appeared in the arsenal of Jew-hatred, valued *Hof-juden*, court Jews, rotted on the gallows of the domains of their princes when the climate of opinion waxed auspicious for revenge on the ethnic progeny of Christ's betrayer. We, too, would eventually find ourselves in line with our people.

My father applied to the Gestapo for exit papers. I went with him. The outcome of a visit to the secret police could not be predicted. Ac-companiment by a young child might just serve as a buffer. But that wasn't needed, not at all. *"Aber lieber Herr Oberrabbiner,"* said the senior officer, rising as we entered, taking my father's hand and pulling up a chair for him. *"Sie wollen uns verlassen!? Warum denn? Dazu gibt's über-haupt keinen Grund! Wir alle kennen Sie doch gut. Sie waren ja immer ein guter, anständiger Mitbürger. Wir halten Sie in Respekt. Sie haben Sich vor garnichts zu fürchten. Wir sind gegen die Ostjuden, gegen die anderen jüd-ischen Schwindler, bestimmt nicht gegen geachtete Juden wie Sie. Bleiben Sie ruhig da, die Aufregungen sind bald vorbei, und dan kehrt alles zum regel-mässingen Zustand zurück."* Then, in broad friendly dialect: *"Na, ja, die Anklage dieser Frau. Die kennt man ja auch! Ist doch a Lügnerin, macht a jedem Schwierigkeiten . . . a unangenehmes Frauenzimmer!"* And, conclud-ing: *"Natürlich, wenn Sie's wollen, haben Sie sofort die Papiere, aber brauchen tun's Sie nicht."*—But my dear Rabbi, you want to leave us? But why? There's no reason for that at all. We all know you well. You've always been a good, decent fellow citizen. We respect you. You have nothing to fear. We are against the Polish Jews, the ones from the East, and the other Jewish swindlers, certainly not against upright Jews like you. Be assured you can stay, the excitement will soon be over, then everything will return to normal. Oh, yes, the accusation by that woman. One knows her. An unpleasant female. Of course, if you want the papers, you'll have them at once, but you really have no need for them.

My father expressed his appreciation, and opted for the documents, just in case, he told the Gestapo man.

Yes, we were exceptionally fortunate those first months. I do not know how many others discovered gentiles of our town who reached out. Undoubtedly, there were some. Some of us who made it to safety could not have done so unassisted. But there were not very many who offered signs of compassion. Had there been more, things might perhaps have stopped short of the ultimate. When it became known that patients in psychiatric hospitals were being put to death by gas or starvation, there was a popular outcry, the churches intervened in strength. The killing stopped. With the exception of a handful of individual priests and pastors, no such intervention was attempted for the Jewish people. Certainly not in Austria. On the contrary. The Germans looked to the Ostmark as a testing ground. How much support would there be for the persecutions? How far could they go? Would there be any demur? The message back was categorical. Carte blanche, no objection. And so, within less than a year, the persecution of the Jews throughout the Third Reich accelerated more than it had in the half decade since 1933 when the Nazis rose to power in Germany. The way lay open to the slide into genocide. The point of no return to the Holocaust is fixed in the map of Austria.

My family left Wr. Neustadt in the early summer. Others were also leaving, the community's structure had crumbled, there was no longer a functioning congregation to be led. We took cover in Vienna, in a large building that also held the offices of the *National Sozialistische Arbeiter Partei,* the Nazi Party. Word had reached my father that the federal Gestapo was looking for him. Prominent Jews were being arrested. The apartment was registered in the name of a couple who had been allowed to emigrate; a hideout under the party's nose seemed more secure than most. My parents did not hazard the streets. Mina, who stayed in Wr. Neustadt, provided necessities and information. It was now urgent that we leave Austria at once. An Aryan family would gain title to the apartment in which we were hiding, and we, its interim, fugitive occupants would be uncovered. But we were trapped. My father's name was added to the Gestapo's list of wanted Jews: The list was checked at all points of exit from the country. My father, born in Pressburg when that city was still within the Austro-Hungarian Empire, had a doubtful claim to citizenship in what had after World War I become the Republic of

Czechoslovakia. There was a chance of winning entrance to Czech territory, but how to get across the border? We waited in the flat, waited not knowing for what precisely, for some breach to be found in the trap. Weeks passed into months, and desperation swelled with the passing days.

Then, late in August, announcements of the search for Oberrabbiner Weiss in black and white in the newspapers, the breach was suddenly there. The doorbell rang, very late in the evening. My father winced, my mother sat still, hands crossed on her lap. At the entrance stood a young man in a black Nazi militia uniform. He extended an arm forward as if to ward something off. *"Herr Oberrabbiner, haben Sie keine Furcht! Ich kam zu helfen."*—Have no fear, Rabbi, I am here to help. "My name is Haslinger. Mina told me where to find you."

Turning to me, he asked: "You remember my young brother from school, don't you? You shared your lunches with him." Then to my parents: "You must all be on the morning train to Pressburg. The Gestapo know where you are. They'll be here by noon tomorrow."

"We can't," said my father. "My name is on a list. They'll take me off at the border."

"No, you will get to Pressburg, I promise you that."

My father cried: *"Unmöglich!* You can't slip through their net. It will be a ride to the Kazett, the concentration camp."

"You have no choice, Oberrabbiner" said the young man. Then he placed his right hand over his left chest, took a step closer, and stared into my father's face: "On my honor, nothing will happen to you. Please be on that train. Please. You will arrive safely."

We took the train. No words were spoken between us. Four suitcases on the small compartment rack. An overnight bag in my father's hand, shirt, underwear, toothbrush and the shaving powder orthodox Jews use instead of a blade, phylacteries. For Dachau. My father was inaudibly reciting *tehillim,* chapters of the Book of Psalms. It was barely an hour from Vienna to the border. I think of that journey as frozen in time, stillness in a glacial cocoon which must not thaw. And then it was broken by a rising, piercing shriek, as of metal grinding against metal, and an acrid smell throughout the carriage of something smoldering. The train had just reached the last stretch before the border, a long easy slope. It should have slowed and halted so that the German-Austrian police could board and make their check, but instead it gathered speed.

A trainman running along the corridor shouted to another something about *die Bremsen,* the brakes. The border post loomed ahead, we raced by it, past gesticulating soldiers and the swastika flag, over a ribbon of empty land, past more soldiers in different garb, past a flagpole with a different flag, coming slowly to a stop several hundred yards into Czechoslovakia. Only Czech gendarmes climbed on. My father's old Czech passport did not pass inspection, but the officer's Slovak was Magyar accented and Hungarian was one of my father's best languages. He joked, a packet of excellent tobacco happened to be in his pocket and why not join him in a pipe while all the fuss was going on outside with the Germans wanting to cross over and the Czechs waving rifles. We were instructed to fill out a temporary visitor's entry form, for three weeks only.

Haslinger was an employee of the Austrian railway system, a militia-man during off-work hours. He had himself assigned to the morning train that day, as brakesman, and whatever it was that he used, it burned out the brakes.

When I went back to Wr. Neustadt in disguise, in 1947, the Haslingers were gone. I have not succeeded in tracing them, even now on this reluctant return to the *Woche der Begegnung.* But back then I learned from Mina that the young man in the black uniform had fallen in the Ukraine.

It has been nearly sixty years, but when I hear a metal surface rasping loud against another he still materializes before me, hand stretched out, hand over heart, word of honor. I am glad that I know nothing of his duties in the East. For what he worked that morning between Vienna and Pressburg I have in thought handed him the *Eisernes Kreuz,* the Iron Cross—metal on metal—that my father won with the Hussars in Transylvania and that now hangs framed together with a 1916 photograph of him, dashing in his uniform, above my desk.

Were I to take the measure of our wretchedness that half year in Nazi Austria, scale it against the evil that blanketed Europe in the time that followed, the reading would barely reach the yardstick's lowest notch. We were not plunged into the First Circle, we had only a glimpse of inferno's anteroom. And yet, as I today conjure up memories of the transformed town and country, an image of Satan and his realm takes shape. The origin of Satan is primeval. It was when nascent Christianity made him incarnate in the body of the Jewish people that his dominion ascended over the affairs of man: the new, crucified deity transubstantiated in the bread of his sacrifice; the Other, the Dark One, in the tribe sufficient in its ancestral covenant; children of the new light arrayed forever against the children of Israel, spawn of Satan, bearers of degenerate DNA. That status has at times been overlaid by a veneer of sufferance, but it has not been revoked. Goethe judged the veneer of civilization on the German nation to be thin and fragile. With the Nazis, it split open. After March 1938, demonization of the Jews soared free of any enshroudment, established—reestablished—as an essential thrust of polity. Austria became a workshop molding an advanced model of Elaine Pagel's conception of Satan's genesis and sway. Demonization, like civilization, is a stepwise process; like all evolution, its pace and bounds are inconstant. Demonization reborn evolved by macrosteps in the Ostmark. We left before it attained unchecked momentum, but the patterns of its progression were there, even if we could not, would not, look unblinkingly ahead to its apotheosis.

We had a three-week period of grace, but not the affidavits and visas to continue on. Friends assured my parents of a better alternative to headlong flight: stay. My father could have any position he wanted, the community would intercede to secure his formal Czech status. Why drift farther into the unknown? What of the old people, the grandmother left behind in Vienna, and here my father's father and aging sisters? Part from them for what would be many years, when really there was no reason to persist with the journey?

Pressburg—Bratislava, now—had all the appearances of normality. Shops bustling, the cafes crowded as ever with their Jewish clientele. What was happening on the other side of the border was terrible, yes, but it would certainly calm down; echoes of the friendly Gestapo chief of Wr. Neustadt. The trouble could not possibly spill over to Czechoslovakia. Anthony Eden had solemnly pledged Britain's commitment to the country's inviolability. Edvard Beneš had declared . . . The French and the Russians were reported to have said . . . Yes, the ethnic Germans of the Sudeten province, enthusiastic Nazis most of them, clamored for union with the Reich, and Germany swore its sacred right to bring the Sudetenland back home. But, after all, the optimists were persuaded, those were not extravagant demands; the Nazis had a point there! When German troops materialized on the far bank of the Danube, facing Bratislava, the optimists concurred that that would be the Germans' final claim. If more palpable encouragement was needed, there were the proud companies of Czech cavalry, sabers flashing, riding up and down the near embankment, the Czech gunboat patrolling our shore!

But Czechoslovakia was beginning to come apart. Other ethnic awakenings. The Slovaks, led by a Catholic priest who seemed to confuse the figure of Hitler with that of Christ returned to earth, insisted on an independent Slovak state. Hungarian irredentists occupied strips of land where the Magyar language was indigenous. My father had ceased to be an optimist. We must move all the way, to America. Without delay. He knew that the need there for middle-aged European rabbis was not exactly pressing, and feared for the family's livelihood. He learned the technique of kasher slaughtering. A fallback position. My mother, who as a girl had studied English, sought to teach him and the children the rudiments of the language. The old ones had to be left behind. They, at least, would not be harmed; one did not yet envisage trains of cattle cars to Planet Death.

The three weeks were up. My father was arrested for overstaying, and released on condition that we depart from Czech territory at once.

We were taken in by the small Jewish community of a village, now in a Hungarian enclave, that had been his first rabbinate, immediately after the war. I joined the Betar youth movement. That was the only time I have found myself on the Right of the political spectrum. Betar was the only Zionist youth group in the village. Wearing the white shirt and blue tie, singing Hebrew songs with other boys, being unabashedly Jewish was intoxicating after the trembling isolation in Wr. Neustadt; late in 1945 I learned that none of those boys survived Auschwitz.

My father gave me lessons in spoken Hebrew, with a bit of Arabic thrown in, just in case. After all, one could not be certain of the final destination.

A huge St. Bernard from the farm where we stayed attached himself to me. When a group of young Hungarian toughs chased me down an alley, Gyöngyös flew at them, teeth bared. I was not bothered again. A thrilling transmutation: the dog, ancient enemy of the Jew at court and in the countryside, now a protector.

But our stopover in Somerein could not last; there was no permit for that, either. For the next months, we moved constantly. Often at night, by horse-drawn carriage and on farm vehicles, passing columns of troops, Hungarians, Slovaks, Czechs. Territories changed hands, boundaries were fluid, sometimes we were unsure into whose control we had strayed. Usually, there was sufficient food, but not always. Once we sheltered for a day in an abandoned trench while unidentified planes crisscrossed the sky. I went scrounging, returning proudly with apples and horseradish root. And whenever a permit for a few days could be procured or bought, back we went to Bratislava and Prague in pursuit of the papers.

In the end, they came through. A cousin who in the 1920s had emigrated and founded a catering business in New York signed the affidavits. My father discovered the whereabouts in Prague of a young woman who had been his student in a course on religion. She was now said to be keeping company with an American consul in the city. She was a stunning lady, she smelled of jasmine, and I was thrilled when, as we left, she drew me close and kissed me on both cheeks. If only she had known sooner, she exclaimed. An American visa . . . no problem, no trouble, she would be delighted. We had the visa two days later. All that remained was to reach a seaport. We had been permitted, while we were still in Wr. Neustadt, to purchase passage to America from monies in the blocked accounts—but only on a German vessel. Traveling through Germany was not possible. The *S.S. Pennland* of the German-American line made stops in Antwerp on her route to New York. Antwerp had to be our next, penultimate destination. Another of my father's cousins was a lumber merchant in Bratislava, dealing largely in hardwoods from the Congo, a fief of Belgium's royal house. We received a transit visa to the port.

Before we left on the flight from Prague, my father took me to the Altneuschul, the fourteenth-century Gothic synagogue. Legend has it that the dust of the Golem lies concealed somewhere in the high, dusky attic. Fashioned from loam centuries ago and invested with life by the great mystic Rabbi Loew, the *Maharal,* the Golem had been his android minion, commissioned to defend Prague's Jews from assault; when the terrifying, looming creature ran wild, the Rabbi had it revert to inanimate earth. The place and the story gripped me. Could I espy the Golem's quiet dust? Could it once more be made alive, just this one time, a shield, a bulwark to us? I have not been back to Prague; the disappointment has sufficed.

People who knew of my father greeted us in Antwerp. Again the temptation. Stay on with us, Oberrabbiner. Whatever may happen there in Central Europe, Belgium is secure. The British. The French. They can't let themselves be outflanked. The Germans can't afford an all-out war. The Maginot Line . . . A pulpit is open for you, Oberrabbiner.

We boarded the *Pennland* the last week of December. The crew behaved correctly. I traded stamps with one of the engineers. On January 4, 1939, we docked in Hoboken, New Jersey. Our combined capital was twenty dollars, our possessions the suitcases, four warm blankets rolled up, and several gold fountain pens bought in Prague, a liquid asset, my father thought. The cousin and his wife were waiting, and newspapermen and photographers, and we were brought to a small furnished flat on New York City's West Side.

My father lived for fifteen years after we came to America, leading his *yeshivah*, before succumbing to the damage done in four years of the Great War on the eastern fronts. He had never been fully well after that, but he worked tenaciously until the week of his death. My mother died a few years later; she had never quite overcome the trauma of dislocation. My sister, who lives in New Jersey, married one of the few survivors of the death factory of Janowska.

Chapter 11

BERKELEY TO JERUSALEM

1965–1967, BERKELEY, CALIFORNIA

I had been on the University of California's faculty of life sciences since 1957. After discharge from military service, I had sought a career in business, a trading house in rare metals, the owner an acquaintance of my father. The American dream of wealth and independence. But the hucksterism and banality of life just north of Wall Street proved intolerable. My mother's expectations fulfilled themselves. I went back to school, earning doctorates in microbiology and in experimental medicine, then postdoctoral years at Rockefeller and in Oxford. There I also achieved the identity of an Anglo-Saxon. The British heard the German accent as one other Yankee savagery; for a few years, it was possible to pass as something I wasn't. Now in Berkeley, I had a research unit of my own, focused on the biology of host-tumor relationships.

Judy and I had a small home in the hills, with almost a view of the San Francisco Bay. We had married young, both still in school. She came from an assimilated Jewish family several generations American. Our three boys grew up taking as natural the privileges of that rare status in the world.

It was an intensive, rewarding period in northern California. Research was exhilarating in the new field of tumor immunology, promotions came fast, funding for the studies was easily acquired. Early mornings out with leathery Nisei fishermen for striped bass off Alcatraz, evenings of cocktails and conspiracy against the nefarious establishment. I was seriously involved with all the correct movements, for free speech on campus, for civil rights, for Chavez and his striking vineyard transients, against the war in Vietnam. I saw those involvements as obligatory, on the *camino real* of the Judaic imperatives of social justice. I had jettisoned religious attachment when, at seventeen, I stumbled onto some texts on geology and evolution and discovered more convincing explanations for the cosmos than those of religion. It took nearly a decade to come to the realization that the defiance had more to do with *Sturm und Drang* and individuation than with metaphysics. The realization forced another return. I tend to excessiveness, and I threw myself into Jewish activities with a vengeance.

There was another realization that insinuated itself into self-awareness, at first only marginally, as I took up the causes of the New Left in Berkeley. It was the unattained need for belonging. I was received into the circle of my academic peers, acknowledged by the students who valued their instructors more for their commitment to the new orthodoxies than for their mastery of knowledge. And yet, a sense of being truly, viscerally integrated in society eluded me.

It has been said that language is the most incontestable *laissez-passer* to belonging. I did not have that pass. My English remained accented, the more so under tension. People have regarded the inflection charmingly European, befittingly cultured. To me it has always been a reminder of a detested place from which I was ejected and to which return was neither possible nor wanted. And a stigma of foreignness. I resented the label I could not cast off, and I still bristle when an opaque listener strains to understand my painstakingly articulated words. I appeared one day with colleagues of the Faculty Free Speech Movement before the City Council of Oakland to plead for yet another permit to demonstrate for or against something or other. An official informed me that the city was not located in Germany, my advocacy out of place and time.

My wife and I had joined CORE, the Congress of Racial Equality. Until it was diplomatically hinted that the struggle best be waged by real Americans.

At the onset of the Cuban missile crisis, groups of patriots let it be known that should the enemy advance on California's borders, the first casualties would be the underminers of the state's Christian American caliber. I had clashed with right-wing hecklers at campus rallies. The calls came in the hours before dawn. "Kike, we're coming for you!"

Others, too, received such greetings, and took them in their stride. I could not. I recalled my father jolting back when the doorbell rang. I bought a .38 Colt. If they came, I would not go lamely.

But it was not that outburst of hatred that tinged the successful Berkeley years with a shadow of tenuousness. Nor was it the Black leaders' rejection of the Jews who, their fervent alliance an expendable quantity, make up the soft underbelly of white society, vulnerable, accessible to assault, like the abdomen of prey to hyenas and Cape hunting dogs. After all, anti-Semitism and racism in all its maskings are pandemic. The sense of isolation derived more from the company of my enlightened comrades in arms. Were we really motivated by the same persuasions, I asked myself when Mao's little Red Book of revelation and the flag of North Vietnam came into view at protests against the war in southeast Asia. I was there not in companionship with Ho Chi Minh but in allegiance with those who were dying in a brutal, senseless conflict.

Estrangement grew stronger in the course of our fevered caucuses. Militancy came to be a contest, radicalness to have a momentum unto itself, its germinal propositions fading, the targets shifting. It was not always easy to tell whether the picket line around the federal building was for nuclear disarmament or for divestment of sexual inhibitions. What mattered was the radical posture. That had its rewards, certainly, in the accolades of the blonde-tressed young women who, like priestesses of a fertility god's shrine urging devotees to ardency, attended on the faculty senate's passionate deliberations. But radicalness as its own end leaves me uneasy. I do have a penchant for assertive noncomformity, but I require orientation. With the points of the compass defined, I can permit myself extravagances of dissent. But Berkeley's avant-gardism was at its heart too amorphous. It did not provide me with a substrate for full-fledged membership in its culture.

Some of the tenor of dislocation remained at the threshold of perception, until my first, unanticipated visit to Israel. But my wife reminds me that long before, I had at moments spoken of alien corn. She remembers my searching the eucalyptus-fringed ridge above our home and asking, of no one in particular, rhetorically only, whether I wanted one day to have my bones resting in this earth. It once belonged to Ishi and his tribe, and then to the stronger people who had come and destroyed them. I was of neither nation. I and my children had drifted into a lovely land to which we were not organic. The passportless cosmopolitan.

That was fine, for a while. But it was without a footing. Only a present, neither a history nor a future of essence.

1965: An invitation from the Academy of Medical Sciences of the U.S.S.R. A select conference on tumor immunology, one of the first scientific workshops with foreign participation, to take place that spring in Sukhumi, in Abkhazia, on the shores of the Black Sea. Twenty-five Soviet researchers, an equal number from abroad, the conference in honor of Professor Zilber, the distinguished Jewish scientist who had been exiled to Siberia and recently was rehabilitated in one of the Soviet dictatorship's tentative thaws. We were to meet in the dacha of the late Lavrenti Beria.

The invitation was appealing, a small plum of recognition. The pioneers of the new discipline would be there. A part of the world I had not come near before. But I hesitated. Give recognition, in return, to an oppressive regime? But then, how oppressive was it, really? Among many circles of the Left, there was still a great deal of denial. It was in the Soviet Union that Jews fleeing before the German onslaught had survived, many of them, at least. It was Soviet troops who liberated the death camps of Poland. Official anti-Semitism, the fate of the Kulaks, the trials that consumed the cadres of the revolution, the frozen Archipelago of Gulag, Ivan Denisovich . . . Eleanor Roosevelt had been there and saw it differently. My wife's parents had acquaintances raised in the early faith of idealistic communism who sat teary-eyed at a performance of the Russian Ballet in Philadelphia and exchanged a prayer, next year in Moscow. How much of what was evil in the Soviet Union was, in fact, a product synthesized of the West's enmity and fear?

I turned to a friend, Abraham Joshua Heschel. It was not Cold War malice, he assured me. The evil was real, very deep and prevalent. But there might be greater reason for me to go than record a refusal of protest. He would make inquiries.

The ambassador of Israel to the United States called on me, then other Israelis who were leading the effort to extricate Jews from the Soviet Union. The effort was clandestine. Jewish emigration was forbidden, and the lines of communication between the Israelis and Soviet Jews were fragile. The Soviet authorities kept members of Israel's legation under tight surveillance, at a distance from the people. My Jewish commitment and involvement were known to the Israelis. Perhaps I could be of some help. Would I stay on for several additional weeks?

What was asked of me had nothing to do with espionage. It was, rather, to make contacts, obtain a direct view of the current ambiguities of Jewish existence, and be publicly, assertively, declarative of my Jewish concerns and convictions. As guest of the Academy, I would have a private car, driver, and guide at my disposal, and a freedom of movement not granted to tourists. No less importantly, I would be carrying passports that would be credited by the Jews who feared contact with strangers. Agents provocateurs of the government were a fact of life in the Jewish communities. But such men were not given to appear at early morning or late evening prayer services with their own phylacteries and *tallith,* did not needle the authorities with the questions I was instructed to ask: Why was no kasher food available at Intourist hotels? Why can I not be taken to Babi Yar to offer *kaddish* for the tens of thousands murdered by the Germans in the ravine? ("You are mistaken, there is no such place!" I was told when I arrived in Kiev.) Why is burial in Moscow's Jewish cemetery no longer "possible"? The authorities would not welcome the intrusions, but the Academy's invitation conferred VIP status, and distinguished guests could reasonably count on a modicum of acquired immunity. Both the American and Israeli consular staffs would know my daily whereabouts and, in any event, I had intelligence experience in the American Army and had learned such elementary skills as identifying and shaking off someone who was tailing me.

So I went, for over three weeks. Sukhumi, villages of Grusinian Jews in Georgia, Kiev, Moscow, Zagorsk. A return to Jewish insecurity startling in its starkness, for all I had learned before the trip. Perhaps not comparable to Austria in the months after the Anschluss, certainly not to what came later as the Third Reich engulfed the European continent. But through the variations of oppression's experience there ran enough of a familiar thread to evoke an anamnestic knowing of the *galut's* precariousness.

I have written elsewhere about those days in Russia and the Ukraine.

The days engendered receptivity for another, unexpected call: a telegram reaching me in Sukhumi from a biologist at the Weizmann Institute who had taken a sabbatical leave in Berkeley. Why not make my maiden trip to Israel before returning to California, if only for a few days, and bring the Institute up to date on what's developing in the field?

Moscow, Warsaw, Vienna. At the airport there, looking for the check-in counter of Austrian Airlines, I was accosted by a man in El-Al flight uniform. He had noticed the El-Al flight bag which I had carried on my shoulder all the miles I had slowly walked through Russian streets and parks, very slowly, the Hebrew letters on the satchel the attractant that might lead to fleeting contact with Jews on bench or corner. Was I traveling to Israel? Yes. Would I instead fly with Israel's airline? He would make the arrangements.

Late night departure. Phylacteries placed on arm and brow at dawn over the Mediterranean. A strangely charged entry into the Holy Land; I have written about that, too. I was driven next day to see Jerusalem, up the old, narrow road winding through the Judean hills. A store of collective, archetypal memories precipitously unearthed. These hills I knew, knew more profoundly than the ones in which I was living in Berkeley, than any others I had ever crossed. Had I not tended a Patriarch's flock on these slopes? Ambushed a Roman legion in a ravine under a Hasmonean's command? Wildly romantic nonsense. Wildly pulling me back. Familiarity not attenuated by the lost millennia. I burst out with that when I met other friends in Jerusalem, scientists I had known at Rockefeller and at Oxford. They laughed. "Are you telling us you have become a convert to Zionism? Careful, there is a madness that hits some people on their first coming to Jerusalem!"

I had not been a Zionist. Nor did I now feel myself following in the footsteps of Theodor Herzl. My thoughts on Zionism were well defined, pat and protective. Another enclave of nationalism in a militantly nationalistic part of the world was not my idea of Judaism's apotheosis. Judaism is above territorial boundaries. A Jew can and must fulfill his mandate of *tikkun olam*—the improvement of the world—wherever fate has landed him. Kalamazoo or Berkeley or the Emek Yezreel. I identified with the exigencies of a displaced people, of course; creation of the state was sheer necessity. I supported that. As a young man I had collected arms for the forces that fought off Arab armies and marauders. But neither politically nor religiously could I be counted in the Zionist camp.

What happened to me on the road to Jerusalem was something else. It was a stunningly personal recovery of the past, a discovery of belonging that had nothing to do with time or language—the Hebrew I knew was liturgical, scholastic, not spoken—and for the first time since the abortive childhood patriotism of Austria there was the plain, overwhelming knowledge of being home.

I stayed for several weeks, made the rounds of universities. If any needed an immunologist or microbiologist, I was there for the taking. If not, there were high schools that surely could absorb another teacher of biology. Language would come. Salary, benefits, facilities . . . all that was of little consequence. It was the hills, the ones that had been mine, not Ishi's.

There were job offers, after all, from universities. I signed on a dotted line, at the Faculty of Medicine in Jerusalem. Even before then, the second day, I cabled the madness to my wife, that I must live in this place. When, later, she acquiesced, it was in the conviction that madness would run its course and pass. Berkeley would take me back. My co-workers were less sanguine. "You are burying your reputation just as you have begun making it," they cautioned. "You'll be starting from scratch, all over again . . . no research moneys, no laboratory set-up, students and assistants to break in . . . it'll be years until you work again . . . and just now the field is taking off." They were right; only that, too, had nothing to do with the case. I did not come into the world with the mandate of breaking new ground in medical research; I was programmed, apparently, to find home. I put a more adult gloss on that, to be part of the great experiment of a people, a nation reborn, a society to be founded on justice and compassion. That was not wholly hyperbole. And there were undoubtedly other motivations. I could not then tease them apart, nor can I today. Friends pointed out that men in their late thirties often feel impelled to a change. A new job, new house, new wife; in my case, a new continent. What I myself recognized was something other. Berkeley had been a testing ground. The areas in which I excelled at school, which drew me, lay in the humanities much more than in the natural sciences. In those, my formal training had been, at best, uneven. I had managed to seek out currents that took me safely between the Scylla and Charybdis of the hardcore, unappealing regimens of mathematics and physics on which modern biomedical science is founded. Later, in research, I compensated with a seemingly innate talent for welding disparate segments of information and ideas into interesting constructs, my beachhead on medicine and science broad but shallow. Somehow, I made it to tenure, a unit of my own, the beginnings of a name as an imaginative, even daring investigator. But I could not shake the sense that I was in constant flight from the more rigorous summons of science. I slid by, very well, but not gallantly, not as my father or Karl May would have met their testing. I should prove myself again, prove my mettle in a harder crucible, fly in the face of the dire warnings of my colleagues.

I could not make the transition to Israel at once; there were responsibilities to research students, time owed the university. In the two years before we could move, the impetuosity of the decision made room for reflection. No matter how forceful the impetus, a return to faraway beginnings also has its reluctances and trepidations. Had I been too impulsive on the drive to Jerusalem? For all its atavistic familiarity, that road also led into an uncharted existence. To what life was I urging my family? Really leave behind all that we had put together here, the good life? I could not entirely disavow the awareness of feeling that I was suspended between two worlds. In the interim, I traveled America crying "Havoc!" about the plight of the Jews in the Soviet Union. I continued in the New Left. And that helped: My activist comrades-in-arms gave resonance to the decision.

Standing in front of the Shattuck Avenue cafe where we had just composed another manifesto of opposition to the war in Vietnam, this time for the ears of the U.N.'s Security Council, one of my comrades, a sociologist, placed his hand on my shoulder, a friendly gesture, and smiled: "Weiss, you know, you really are not fooling anyone. You can say what you want . . . I know exactly what you really are. It's obvious. You are a monarchist!"

Without thinking, instinctively, I shot back something I had never quite put so plainly into words: "You are right, at the court of *Melech Malche Ha'm'lachim*—the King of Kings."

I would have preferred a less crystalline identification, by others, by myself, an amorphousness of loyalties and commitments that gives maneuverability. But, ultimately, if one finds oneself cornered into taking a stand, a very narrow corner, and cannot sneak through like an aberrant cell evading immune surveillance, this was more irreducibly my identity than any other.

In the weeks preceding the Six Day War, Israel's existence turned acutely precarious. Arab armies massed. The Straits of Tiran were shut by the Egyptians. The Third Jewish Commonwealth did not seem strong enough to hold the line; it would fall, in still another genocidal chaos. I tried, with growing desperation, to muster support. Symbolic support, that was all that was possible. I suggested to the Faculty Peace Committee that it would be an appropriate gesture to send a resolution to the White House or Congress or the U.N. attesting our belief in Israel's right to live. The suggestion was dismissed; irrelevant to our goals. How could that be, I contended? We had not been limiting our advocacy to free speech on campus and withdrawal from Vietnam. There had been an outpouring from us of briefs and resolutions for the endangered of the world, in South America, South Africa, the Far East. Surely, the inhabitants of Israel who faced the threat of extinction are not less worthy of the sympathies of this distinguished assembly of scholars? I pleaded. A statement. Something like that, at the right moment, might just have had some effect when other Jews, in other countries, not so very long ago, were imperiled.

Leon Wofsy, the chairman of my division at the University, had been a leading member of the Communist Party until his sentiments for the Hungarians who were crushed by Russian tanks in 1956 caused him to pause and resign. A Jew himself, members of his family lost in the Holocaust and Stalin's purges of the Jewish intelligentsia, he tried. Perhaps, he proposed, we could add a codicil to the next statement on Vietnam. . . . We oppose military violence wherever it takes place, also in the Middle East.

The upper room of the cafe, the site of our cabals, was still. The two dozen academicians searched their pizzas and salads. Peter Scott, who professed one of the humanities, looked uncomfortable, cleared his throat, thought better of it, and merged into the silence. Somebody proposed a comparative analysis of the depths of narrow sea passages. Berkeley's mathematician laureate, Steven Smale, was more forthright, only he had his numbers wrong. Facing me, he said something to the effect that, yes, it is too bad about a couple of hundred thousand Jews in Israel, but what mattered was the national liberation movement of the Third World, of the Arab People. I cried: "There are a couple of million!" One of the things I have not forgiven myself for is that I kept my fists at my side.

I left. I did not return there. From then, I was a stranger openly. By choice. No ambivalence. Less than a year later my wife and children were learning Hebrew in an *ulpan* in Netanya, and I stayed in an immigrant hostel not far from the medical school in Jerusalem, entering my apprenticeship in comprehending the labyrinthine ways of functioning at the institution they called the University of the Jewish People.

Chapter 12

PATER JOHANNES VRBECKY

MAY 1994, JERUSALEM

I had for some time been in correspondence with Felix Szolcsanyi, a Wr. Neustadt journalist. He had set out to write a history of the town's Jewish community as it was in the years before its destruction with the Anschluss. It was to be not merely an academic exercise. Szolcsanyi is a relentless foe of Nazism and racism, and he is fearless in giving voice to his convictions. When Wr. Neustadt with great fanfare and festivity commemorated the 800th anniversary of its founding he reported that "in all the pomp, not a syllable spoken, not by anyone, of the Jews who for hundreds of years contributed to the town's flourishing. . . . But that hardly surprises me. . . . In the last elections, Jörg Haider's nationalists became Wr. Neustadt's second strongest party. . . ." He added a reflection to the account: "There is no memorial to Neustadt's murdered gypsies. The plaque marking the site where the synagogue stood has to this day not been dedicated. Erosion and pollution continue unchecked the work of decay of the Jewish cemetery. The names of many murdered Jews and communists are missing on Neustadt's monument to the victims of fascism. And the town's authorities found nothing amiss in naming a street for the poet Ernst Wurm who in the dark times worked for the Nazi propaganda sheet, the *'Völkischer Beobachter'*." In an accompanying article, Szolcsanyi barely curbed his outrage: "Unbelievable, but true. The picture of Mayor Edmund Scheidtenberger, the Nazi who reigned as dictator over Wr. Neustadt from 1938 to 1945, hangs to this day in the Gallery of Honor on the second floor of City Hall." When in response to protests by a Socialist youth group and the small local Anti-Fascist Committee, the picture was finally taken down, it was, the town's present mayor Dr. Peter Wittmann informed Szolcsanyi, "because it had to be moved to the Archives during restoration of the hall's peeling paintwork." Scheidtenberger was odious even for a Nazi functionary. "Fifty years after the war," Szolcsanyi fumed in a letter to me, "a young Socialist mayor cannot find the critical words to distance himself from the Nazi past . . . that left Neustadt with seventeen houses standing. . . . The words could cost him too many votes."

One portrait of my hometown today.

Szolcsanyi's work was to be anchored in the personal testimonies of Wr. Neustadt's dispersed Jewish survivors. He had traced a number of us, and then learned from a physician at Stanford, a friend of my parents whom I had known professionally in my Berkeley days, that I, too, was among the living.

I received a letter from an unknown writer, Mag. P. Johannes Vrbecky, Prior, the Neukloster in Wr. Neustadt. Originally a Dominican church and convent, the Neukloster was gifted by Friedrich III to the Cistercian Order in 1444. I had known the imposing Gothic edifice as a child, from a distance. It was not a place Jewish children cared to loiter about. Chances were a stone would be thrown by one of their kids on the way to or from Mass. . . . *Et cum spiritu tuo.*

Pater Vrbecky wrote that he was preparing for his next trip to Israel when one of his former students, Felix Szolcsanyi, came to ask him about a tombstone fragment that had surfaced during foundation repairs on one of the town wall's towers. Was the stone's inscription Hebrew, as Szolcsanyi surmised? The Prior had studied the language as a seminarian, but that was long ago, and although he was certain the characters were Hebrew script he could not decipher them. Perhaps, Szolcsanyi suggested, the Oberrabbiner's son in Jerusalem could help.

Pater Vrbecky went on to introduce himself. Three years younger than I, he had studied for the priesthood at the Cistercians' convent in Heiligenkreuz and had been priest at the Neukloster for most of his years since ordination. He mentioned his various positions—chaplain, dean, prior—but wryly added these were not to be taken as titles, but, rather, as euphemisms for bothersome bureaucratic assignments. He described a Jewish connection, discovered only after many years in Wr.

Neustadt. His uncle had been married to a Jewish woman, the sister of an attorney on the town's police force. The sister's family *"wurden im KZ umgebracht"*—were murdered in the concentration camp. The attorney's daughter had escaped to England. Vrbecky had located her, a friendship developed, she had visited him at the Neukloster. The visit had been *"für mich sehr berührend, denn da tat sich für mich ein Stück meiner eigenen Geschichte auf"*—"for me very emotional, because it opened for me a piece of my own history."

The straightforwardness was surprising. This was no less a personage than the lord of an ancient enemy's keep! What he went on to write was even more perplexing. He had been to Israel many times, both as leader of church groups and alone, incognito, "to learn the country and its people not as tourist but as observer. . . . I realize that there is nowhere an exclusive 'world of grace,' not in Rome, not in Jerusalem, not anywhere else. . . . The basis of our faith is fused of many components: history, religion, patterns of living, archeology, the past, and the present. The New Testament too is a Jewish book, which can truly be understood only in relation to Judaism. . . . I want to know Judaism at its core, its origins. I have read something about Judaism, have a bit of biblical knowledge, but I must gain deeper insight into all the links. They are of great importance to me, because in Judaism there lies the basis of our belief in God, . . . the basis of our being human, of the understanding of our existence." He is quite independent, he does not wish to impose— he emphasizes that—but he would be grateful if I "could spare a bit of time for a short personal contact."

So I become guide to the Jewish people in their land for an Austrian Cistercian who sometimes reads Mass wearing a *tallith* and seeks in Judaism the context for his priesthood and humanity.

I went to meet him in the lobby of the Hotel Ariel, not far from the Temple Mount. A somewhat heavy, florid man, thinning gray hair, dressed in casual slacks and sweater, I spotted him at once, bent over a book on his lap. Unmistakably a priest, I thought, and then wondered if that would have occurred to me had I not known whom I was to meet.

Over the next days, we were together for many hours. Walking the thronged neighborhoods of premodern Jerusalem—the Bokharian Quarter, the Nachlaoth, Musrarah; stopping at the intimate Sephardi prayer houses with their cushioned benches arrayed to form a square around the raised platform and lectern from which the Torah is read, the walls decked with framed excerpts of the liturgy, some in ornate kabbalistic patterns; passing through a time warp into hasidic shtetls resurrected and transposed to David the King's capital—Mea Shearim, Bate Hungaria, Geulah—redolent alleyways, their walls plastered with crying calls to female modesty and the most recent exhortations of the rebbes to relentless piety; men in black *kapotes* and the head coverings and high stockings that distinguish each master's followers rushing feverishly between *shtiblach* and *yeshivoth,* not really seeing us but, rather, looking through the stranger toward something that would transcend the material; women and young girls hurrying about female tasks, some so wholly covered in drab wrappings that only the face can be discerned, their womanhood closed off from the eyes of the passing beholder, others incongruously got up smartly, makeup and elegant *sheitels* that almost can be mistaken for a girl's native hair but femininity nonetheless at a remove from nature's spontaneity; the bearing of these people speaking of an enlistment in the service of a seclusive, beleaguered holiness. Into the sprawling, pullulating open market of Mahane Yehudah where all the concurrent worlds of this city brush against each other, as people of all classes rub shoulders in an English pub; here in the raucous confrontations of the Middle East between purchaser and supplier of everything that flesh and spirit can want, the incredibly varied mainstays and luxuries of household and table and the appurtenances of religious observance. Back to the Jerusalem of the late twentieth century, the facades of Jerusalem stone glowing in the late afternoon's refracted pastels, grand synagogues that could well have stood in the places he knew, Vienna or Graz or Wr. Neustadt, museums, memorials to all that has taken place here and in the millennia's wanderings of the Jewish people, Yad Vashem where Johannes Vrbecky had been before but not with someone who would unravel its litanies of life and death.

By the second day, an unspoken understanding: The "Sie" was an artifact, a formality of address ingrained in German culture, even among old friends, but suddenly incongruous in what we were about. We became "Du," Johannes, David, and the gaps of so many centuries had shrunk to the space between two aging men walking a route of commonality.

Friday, dusk. *Kabbalath Shabbath,* the bidding welcome to the Queen of the Sabbath, at the synagogue in Rehaviah of which we and our children have been part since settling in the city. It is called *Ha'zvi Yisrael.*

Those are the opening words of David's lament for Saul and Jonathan fallen in battle against the Philistines, "Thy beauty, O Israel, is slain upon your high places; how are the mighty fallen!" At the sanctuary's entrance there is affixed a simple plaque with the names of the twenty-eight boys and girls who have died in modern Israel's wars and border skirmishes. It is a rather small community.

Rehaviah is upper middle class and professional, and a disproportionate number of *Ha'zvi*'s congregants are prominent in academia, law, medicine. The synagogue is orthodox, of a centrist, enlightened bent. Introductions. Johannes was received warmly. He was not the first Christian clergyman to be with us for Sabbath prayers; there have been others, members of Jerusalem's many ecclesiastic orders and institutions, students at the university. After the service and at the Sabbath table in my home, discussions with scholars of Jewish law and philosophy. Origins, things in common, and divergence. He was ecstatic. This is what he had been seeking in Israel, he told me again and again, links. Johannes was teaching religion at Wr. Neustadt's classical gymnasium, where once my father taught. He has assembled a collection of Jewish ceremonial objects; his students must know that their faith's covenant is inseparable from another, ancient one that has perdured, and they must appreciate its celebrations. But this Sabbath eve Johannes was with people for whom the symbols and the essence have a vital cogency and for the first time he could fully apprehend their range and depth.

Sunday, at Kibbutz Palmach-Zova. My friend there, Yaakov Hatzubai, who as a child survived the annihilation of Hungary's Jews and had been brought to Israel in a children's transport and later fought in the Palmach, now is my companion when we hike the country's trails and swamps and ridges, north to south, east to west, the soles of our feet affirming an inseparability from the earth to which we had come back. The priest seemed to understand that our circuits were more than love of nature, that they held us—Yaakov the agnostic, me the romantic who no longer could shake off belief—in a shared mystique.

There is an underground spring at Zova that seeps out of the bedrock and collects in a pool at the base of a high, arched chamber of hewn stone, the water flowing out from there through a long, very low narrow tunnel to the tiered orchards below. Men fashioned the waterworks in the times of the kings of Judea, perhaps even earlier. To reach the vault, one must slither down a circular, vertical shaft of molded rocks, the passage just sufficient for an average person's width. One of my sons spent the bachelor's night before his wedding down there, with friends from his religious youth movement, playing the pioneers' old songs on his guitar through the night. Now, Johannes was to make the descent. He hesitated a moment, contemplating his girth and the diameter of the shaft, and thought it just possibly a go. Puffing, scraped, and triumphant, he made it. Down below, we talked of how the land's milk and honey had always to be wrested from its parched limestone and granite, that the promised land had never been an easy one, that trickles of water were its life. We talked of the deities of nature and fertility that had been worshipped in ancient Canaan, and of the deadly enmity borne them by the invading Israelite tribes and their single jealous God. Then we made our way up into the evening and had supper in the kibbutz dining room.

The day after he returned to Wr. Neustadt, Johannes called. He had taken with him bottles of kasher wine and brandy from Ben-Gurion airport, and at Siegel's, the iron dealers on the ground floor of the house where my family had lived on the *Hauptplatz*, he had bought two sets of dishes, pans, and cutlery. A corner of the *Neukloster*'s kitchen was being set aside for their keeping. The cook was going to Vienna to be instructed in the ways of kasher cooking by the rabbi's wife. A room in the monastery was mine, whenever I would accept his invitation to come. I had explained to Johannes that that was out of the question. He understood that well, he assured me when we parted, but nonetheless, just perhaps, if somehow, at some time . . . I would be awaited and I would be met with love.

Chapter 13

HILLEL AND YAIR SIGN ON

MAY 1995, JERUSALEM

F riday night dinner at my oldest son's home. Hillel is a clinical psychologist; he also commands an infantry battalion in the reserves. Earlier this year, he and other young officers founded a new *minyan*—a prayer group—that meets Sabbaths and holidays in the study hall of a girl's school near where he lives in Ba'aka. That evening, his oldest child, Yair, who had just turned twelve, led *kabbalath shabbath* services. Musical talent has skipped two generations in my family. My father had a resonant tenor voice; he was as stirring a *ba'al t'fillah*—cantor—as he was an orator. I, in deafening contrast, am told that I invariably manage to falsify by the third bar of a tune, and two of my three sons have inherited the failing. Since my thirteenth birthday, I have resisted every invitation to lead a service or song; that would be an infliction on the hearers. The talent has again come to the fore in Yair. I congratulated him on his maiden appearance before the arc. Then I said:

"You know, Yair, two weeks from tonight, I will be conducting my first *kabbalath shabbath*, in the place where I grew up. Because your great-grandfather was the rabbi, and there may not be anyone else who remembers how the prayers go." Helmuth and Uli had arranged for the returning Wr. Neustädters to meet the Queen of the Sabbath at the only Jewish site left, the row of tombstones embedded in the town wall.

My son and his wife exchanged a glance. Then Hillie said:

"No, you won't, dad. I will. I am coming, too, I have your father's name. And Yair will help me, he is the one with the voice. You can give the speeches."

I had had no intimation of this. Hillie tends to taciturnity. But he had made his plans. He was to be on maneuvers the week of the return, but his second-in-command would take over for a few days; Hillie would pick up his son on the way from the field to the airport and arrive in Austria two days late. He would bring a tape recorder and video camera. He has often maintained that I have told him little of my youth, his grandparents, our lives before the Germans arrived. That has always come as a surprise to me. I thought I had related a great deal to my children; apparently there can be large gaps in the absorbing of history casually transmitted and passively received. Hillie and his brothers identify strongly with the family and its past and with the Holocaust's legacy, but that seems to be more a sensibility than a knowing. Now, in the landscape of memory, knowing would take on clarity. He called Joshua and Jeremy. They couldn't free themselves; Hillie would be the representative. He would ask the survivors of Wr. Neustadt's Jews to fill in the blanks of his family's story.

My wife decided to remain behind. It was the descendants of the rabbi who alone, unencumbered, should make this journey. For them, the return was more than a community's response to the reaching out of a remarkable Christian congregation. It was a personal quest to bring the memory of forebears alive in the continuum of the line.

The Eiwens were delighted that three generations of one household would be represented. A return in depth; another sign of God's hovering grace over the remnants of His people's exile.

I purchased the flight tickets for myself and Hillie and Yair in Jerusalem. I did not want to accept that largesse from Ichthys, and I was still on guard: I had to assure myself the decision was, finally, mine.

Pastor Helmuth Eiwen and his wife, Uli, during the
Week of Return, May 1995.

Reception in Wiener Neustadt City Hall during the Week of Return.
Left to right: Mayor Peter Wittmann, Pater Johannes Vrbecky, David Weiss.

Friday night service facing thirteenth-century Jewish tombstones embedded in the medieval city wall of Wiener Neustadt. David Weiss explains the meaning of the Sabbath. Seated are the Israelis who returned for the week. Standing around them are members of the Ichthys community and other local Christians. May 1995.

David Weiss's grandson, Yair, and son, Hillel, conduct the Friday night service.

Children of the Ichthys community youth group perform Jewish and Israeli dances for the returning Israelis at the community's meeting house, May 1995.

Group photograph of the returning Israelis, in front of the Ichthys community meeting house, May 1995.

A plaque designed by Carola Tengler of the Ichthys community, set into the city wall adjacent to the thirteenth-century Jewish tombstones. The legend below the citation from Isaiah ("Comfort ye, comfort ye, my people . . .") reads: "Jewish citizens who had to leave this town in 1938 return as survivors and once more celebrate the Sabbath. May 6, 1995—Ijar 5755."

Marianne Neuber, professor at the Realgymnasium in Wiener Neustadt, with daughter Nina, at Purim party, 1998, in Bat Yam high school during exchange visit to Israel by Wiener Neustadt pupils.

David W. Weiss at Massadah, overlooking the Dead Sea, 1998.

Chapter 14

THE WEEK OF RETURN: WIENER NEUSTADT, MAY 1995

MAY 21–28, 1995. DIE WOCHE DER BEGEGNUNG

Other portraits of my hometown today, mixed media.

SUNDAY

Giving In Too Easily?

We are met as we arrive, in small groups and individually, at the airport in Schwechat on Vienna's outskirts. Counting several husbands and wives who do not stem from Wr. Neustadt, we are a contingent of forty, Israelis and a handful of Americans; an elderly crowd, I in my late sixties among the youngest. For the first time in more than fifty years, I am again called Schatzi.

Almost all of us are from families with roots in the Seven Communities. We grew up in orthodox households, but only a few have sustained the commitment. The orphaned children who reached Palestine were often placed in left-wing Socialist *kibbutzim* and weaned from all connection with the despised *galut*, the Diaspora, the land to give them rebirth as the new Jew, free, proud, the pioneer. Israel's society has retained certain affinities for the tradition and some of its celebrations, but only a minority of its people accept the patterns of meticulous observance. The Eiwens had inquired what heed they should take of Jewish dietary regulations in planning their hospitality. Knowing that most of us did not adhere to these, and that a *kasher* kitchen had been unknown in Wr. Neustadt since the dispersion of the Jews after the Anschluss, I thought a minimalist response to their concern satisfactory. I, myself, have no problems of conscience living *"milchig tref"* when I travel, avoiding forbidden items but disregarding the many ancillary demands of the rules of *kashruth*. If dairy and vegetarian dishes are available, the requirements of all of us would certainly be met. But I underestimated. Lily Schischa and a few others and then my son let me know they could take no such liberties with the law. Somewhat impatiently, I advised that they bring preserved food along from Israel; there is a limit to how much we can impose on the generosity of our hosts! I underestimated again, this time Ichthys. They have great respect for Judaism and God's commandments to the Jews. At the airport Helmuth informs me, casually, that our meals at the hotel and at all functions and events will be delivered daily to Wr. Neustadt by a *kasher* caterer in Vienna. "But that must cost much more!" I protest. Helmuth won't relate to that. "We have brought you back as Jews," is his reply.

We exit immigration and customs, and there they are, the Eiwens' people, with bouquets of flowers, waving small Israeli flags, many youngsters among them. Shalom, shalom. We are each taken in hand by a family, given *Kaffee mit Schlag und Torte*—coffee with whipped cream and cake—and then driven to our hotel, the Corvinus, in Wr. Neustadt.

My reception is more complicated. There are Helmuth and Uli and some of their children, and there are also Pater Johannes and Toni Macheiner. Over our drinks I find myself in an uncustomary position, holding fracture lines of Christian antagonism from breaking open. The return is sponsored wholly by the Pentecostal sect. In his letters Johannes has emphasized that, for all his personal support of the idea, neither he nor any other Catholic churchman can participate. There can be no communion between Christ's establishment and its plebeian dissidents. Johannes is at Schwechat only as my friend. He and the Eiwens have not previously met. They have spoken by phone to coordinate the *Woche*'s program with plans Johannes has for my stay. The coordination proves faulty. I am the rabbi's son, the spokesman, and the Eiwens have set me a formidable schedule of talks and gatherings. So, it turns out, has Johannes. I have accepted his invitation to stay at the Neukloster. But I have returned to Wr. Neustadt because of the Eiwens and Ichthys. Fall short of the role I so reluctantly accepted and that is now in earnest friendship claimed by divided camps? We work out a double agenda; that will take two additional days if I am not to slip on the razor's edge of dissonant calls to revive a Jewish presence in a town that won fame for its detestation of Jews.

Toni drives Johannes and me to Wr. Neustadt. Several months earlier I spoke in Jerusalem, at the King's Hotel, to a group from Johannes's parish; late that evening, they formed a circle around me in the lobby and chanted the ancient priestly blessing "May God bless you and keep you, may He shine his face upon you . . ."; Toni Macheiner was one of them. Now, he is grumbling about the Eiwens' arrogation of ownership of my time and person. Our first stop is at Dr. Stiglbauer's, a Neukloster parishioner. He is a year younger than I am; I did not know him as a child. His brother I recall well. He was the class bully, the one I managed in a flurry of heroism to throw to the wooden, oiled classroom floor; he had taunted me, in his crisp *Hitler Jugend* uniform that I feared and envied, and I had lost control. I am taken to the Stiglbauers to see their collection of Wr. Neustadt memorabilia. Lithographs, paintings, old plans of the town, antique artifacts. More coffee and cake and graciousness after the initial awkwardness of meeting. The doctor is also an avid botanist. His shelves are crowded with portfolios of prints of the world's flora. He asks my assistance: He has heard of a grapefruit-like fruit, the pomello, which grows in the Jordan Valley and other parts of Israel. But he knows little about the plant and has no picture. Can I enlighten him? I do the best I can; when I come home, I will ask Joshua to take photographs of the pomello in a citrus plantation near Nechalim, his *moshav.* No one mentions the dark years. The hour passes quickly. On the way to the Neukloster, I am aware that this was a pleasant visit, my first in Wr. Neustadt. I have let my guard down too much, my reserve. These are not Ichthys people. I shall have to be more careful. I have not come to enjoy *Gemütlichkeit.*

The Neukloster: We pass through the somewhat dilapidated cloisters, weeds and peeling paint on the facades, ascend to a high second story, and down the corridor; several doors distant from Johannes's apartment there is the long, narrow room that is mine. A tall feather bed, closets cleared for the new occupant, a working table with all the paraphernalia of stationery, a sink with overhanging shelves on which new toilet articles are arrayed. There is no crucifix on the wall. A small eighteenth-century silver menorah, *Alt-Wien*, has been placed on the coffee table. The room is lit by a huge double window which faces an immense, overgrown meadow, once a lawn, to which one descends, from the ground floor, by a curving balustraded staircase that I judge to be baroque; the stone's edges are smoothly indistinct where generations of monks have made their way down to pace in the walled grounds. I am given keys to my room, to the modern bathroom at the far end of the corridor, and to the monastery's portals. Then I am welcomed by Frau Piribauer, the mistress of the kitchen who was sent to learn the arcana of *kashruth,* and by her handyman husband. More graciousness. Then Johannes escorts me, a short walk through estranged, familiar streets, past the Kapuzinerkirche and the Rodelberg whose precipitous slopes I had dared with my sled but which seems to have shrunk to a gentle mound barely two men's height, to the Corvinus, where our first gathering with Ichthys is to take place.

Supper together in one corner of the dining room. I wear a handknit gray *kippah,* a gift from one of my daughters-in-law; I shall wear it constantly this week. Elazar Ben-Yoetz, the youngest among us—he was a few months old when his family fled—has donned a large black one. The diners at tables on the far side regard us curiously as the waiters serve the *kasher* meals in plastic trays. I notice several men moving in and out of the room and the adjacent lobby, scanning the premises and the comers and goers. They are detectives from the federal bureau of security; six of them are assigned to us for the week, Helmuth tells me. They will at night patrol the floors on which our rooms are located and accompany us in unmarked cars on all trips planned for our stay. I speak with the one who seems in charge. He assures me there is no cause for alarm, just a precaution, not a bad idea, he thinks. Not long ago a building in the town's vicinity that housed gypsies was firebombed, there were casualties, *das Gesindel hat man noch nicht erwischt*—the hoodlums have not yet been caught—and there are still people around with the old ideas about Jews.

We are joined by Helmuth and Uli and others of the congregation. They are radiant. God has brought us here, they are only His agents; His hand is so plainly at work this evening. Some have again brought their children. The teenagers seem as excited as their parents. I am charmed by Brigitte, the Eiwens' sixteen-year-old daughter; she is a leader, with her tomboyish ebullience and mischievous eyes, unabashedly greeting the strangers and running about the gardens with her pack. Short speeches of welcome by Helmuth and Uli, and a rundown of our activities for the coming days. They have succeeded in wedging cracks in the boycott of their group, at least for the occasion of our return. There will be *Begegnungen* with a Catholic Workers Circle and with Aktion Mitmensch, a human rights fellowship, at the St. Bernhard educational center in the Neukloster complex; the mayor will host an official reception; we shall meet with students of the Bundesrealgymnasium; we will be given a tour by the archivist of the museum and of the town's once "Jewish sites"; there will be a formal luncheon in Vienna given by the regional government of Niederösterreich; perhaps still other functions as the thaw induced by the unwonted Jewish presence might spread. God's hand at work.

The meal over, the Ichthys people gone home, we sit on the hotel's patio; all of us, I think, somewhat dislocated in time and place. The hotel stands at the edge of a garden path that leads into the *Stadtpark*. The path's other side is bordered by the town wall. From the patio we look directly across to the Jewish tombstones. Only a few feet farther along, a cage holding two black bears is fastened against the wall; the animals appear forlorn in their cramped quarters. An incongruity that strikes me, perhaps unfairly, as culturally atavistic; bear-baiting and Jew-baiting were not so very long ago among the town's amusements.

There is a motif to our conversation this soft evening in late May, a question which each one of us has posed and to which the answer has remained ambiguous. Why, finally, did we return? Some have been back before, to the cemeteries of Wr. Neustadt and the villages of the Burgenland; some to tread the streets of our youth, as I felt compelled to do when I came in disguise from my unit in Germany. A few had encountered naked hatred. Willie Reininger, whose family found refuge in Montevideo, had stood in front of what had been their house. Neighbors had come out and taunted, *"Na, ja, da steht wieder solch einer . . . die Reininger Juden wollen das Haus zurück . . . die können schon d'rauf warten!"*—"So, here one of those is standing again . . . the Reininger Jews want their house again . . . they're gonna have to wait for that!" What really are we doing here now? Yes, we were triggered by the irresistible sincerity of the Eiwens. But another reason has taken shape during the past months. An assertion, a defiance, not yet fully conscious, not verbalized. Pride. Israeli pride. And, more deeply, pride in the indestructibility of the Jewish people; a Jewish community's witness to continuity in the place where it was to have ended. This will be the theme to run through my talks. But how, with my limited vocabulary in the language, can I avoid a jarring dissonance with the admiration so justly due our extraordinary hosts? I have with me Langenscheidt's German-English dictionary, but that cannot be drawn from a pocket at moments of truth. I have never been able, on any topic, in any framework, to read a prepared lecture. When I've tried, the sentences come out wooden, dead. I learned decades ago that I can only speak spontaneously, once having thought things out; then the talk is alive and the words penetrate. I resolve to put the dictionary away, to return semantically to the first ten years of my life; that will have to do.

We share as well an embarrassment until now not quite admitted, a recurrent suspicion of ourselves, and of our hosts. We confess that to each other this evening. Have we given in too easily? Where were all these good people back in 1938? That many of them were then not yet in the world, the others only children, that is a matter of logic, but the feelings of pain and loss as we reenter our own childhoods are not altogether rational, they are also rooted in the searing emotions of collective recall.

What we do not, cannot, know this evening is that another feeling will rise to undeniable tangibility, side by side with scorching memory: Friendship. With another, small collective, the people in this place who *have* taken a stand.

MONDAY

Where the Temple Stood

Breakfast at the Neukloster with Johannes, Pater Otto, and Pater Roman. The refectory is a large, elongated room, the walls illuminated by late Renaissance frescoes, the ceiling timbered. The hall is used for parish affairs and by the few resident monks; most of the Cistercian community now reside at the order's mother monastery in Heiligenkreuz. Pater Otto is a short, diffident, very gentle man in his mid-eighties. He carried on with his priestly functions during the war years; not, I gather, regarded an admirer of the regime, he was on several occasions interrogated by the Gestapo. Pater Roman, tall, slim, outgoing, was ordained only some years ago. He gives me his card: *"Durch die Gnade Gottes, Priester Jesu Christi, P. Roman Nägele, Benediktiner von St. Georgenberg-Fiecht"*—"By the Grace of God, Priest of Jesus Christ, Benedictine . . ." On the reverse side, a photograph of a thirteenth-century icon, dark as the Czestochowa Madonna, a Nordic Christ hanging from the cross. Pater Roman is assigned as chaplain to the Neukloster; the Cistercian order has ties to the order founded in the early sixth century by St. Benedict.

Platters of cheese, butter, and brown bread on the heavy oaken table that stretches the length of the room. My place is set with a fresh mat, a color different from the others, and with a new plate and cutlery. I am asked to recite the blessing over the bread and grace after the meal, in the Hebrew of the Jewish prayer book; I will have that honor throughout my stay.

There is some excitement. Yesterday morning, in the course of his sermon at Mass, Johannes expressed his joy at the visit of "his special friend, the son of Wr. Neustadt's last rabbi." Later in the day, a swastika was sprayed on one of the cloister's inner piers. The Piribauers have scrubbed the wall, only a dark smudge remains. The *Wiener Neustädter Nachrichten* has reported the incident. The suspect is a teenager, and the article's byline ponders whether the desecration was *"von Judenhassern angestiftet"*—instigated by Jew-haters. The monks and the detectives who have come to investigate prefer to believe the memento to have been the work of a disturbed boy, one known to the police, a petty vandal.

We stand assembled, our group of returnees, facing a building on the Baumkirchnerring, in the center of town, not far from the Hauptplatz. The building houses offices. A brass plaque at the entrance identifies the site: This is where the *Tempel* stood. We are silent. There is nothing to say at this moment, it seems. What stood here was a point of convergence of our young lives. What stands now, neat and orderly, is a usurpation born in violence. When I was last in Wr. Neustadt, nearly forty years ago, the shell of the *Tempel* was still erect, the frontage as it was since its defacing by the S.A. in the *Kristallnacht,* the interior eviscerated, a depot for a lumber company. In a way, I think, that was easier. One can cry at the ruins of a beloved place. Even God does, the Talmud holds:

> It has been taught: Rabbi Jose says, I was once traveling on the road, and I entered into one of the ruins of Jerusalem in order to pray. The Prophet Elijah appeared . . . and said to me: My son, what sound did you hear in this ruin? I replied: I heard a divine voice, cooing like a dove, and saying: Woe to the children, on account of whose sins I destroyed My house and burnt My temple and exiled them among the nations of the world! . . . Woe to the father who had to banish his children, and woe to the children who had to be banished from the table of their father!

One might even find comfort. Rubble betokens a past and challenges a restoration. In a shell the spirit of something sacred, of something dear, can reverberate, can be felt. But tears in contemplation of a trade union's bureaus? In that, there is no seed of renewal. Only a dry absence.

Our guide is Dr. Beatrix Bastl, the town's archivist. She is young and energetic. She knows the history of Jewish Wr. Neustadt, and her understanding of the tortuous paths that tore us from here and brought us back for these days is unmistakable, an unspoken concordance.

We go to the Jewish cemetery. The gate to the enclosure is locked. Someone brings the key. The section of the burial ground that has been left is well kept. Only a few of the graves are of relatives of our group— most of them lie in the graveyards of the Seven Communities—but this small plot of land was our community's. It is also a collective, of the dead, and we move along the rows and recite *kaddish*, the men with *kippoth* that do not seem awkward on heads unaccustomed to their wear.

Another sepulcher, a corner on the museum's second floor where the town's Judaica is on sight. Glass-topped showcases display medieval Hebrew manuscripts, deeds of mercantile transactions, records of communal and family events. Brackets on the walls hold tombstone fragments, a bas-relief of unknown provenance purported to be the image of ancient Jerusalem's High Priest, and the *Judenspott,* the carving of the reclining sow and her suckling rabbis.

Dr. Bastl hopes to enlarge the museum's Jewish section. She would like to bring it up to date, up to the Anschluss, to document a more recent Jewish presence than that which Maximilian I so peremptorily terminated. She asks us for whatever we can send her, photographs, letters, diaries, newspaper clippings.

We arrive at the Allerheiligenplatz, the heart of the medieval Jewish quarter. A small, busy square, shops, cafes, crowds milling about. The one Jewish remnant is a house, cramped in a row of others, that was home to Rabbi Israel Isserlein, the great fifteenth-century talmudic scholar and communal leader. Shmuel Givon, one of the Hacker brats, now turning seventy, who commanded crack regiments in Israel's wars, is a painter and sculptor at the artists' colony of Ein Hod. He makes an offer: to create an imposing memorial for the square, fashioned of fieldstone from the Galilee. Dr. Bastl thinks the idea splendid; so do our Ichthys hosts when Shmulik repeats his proposal. Most of our group are skeptical. We doubt the undisturbed longevity of a Jewish memorial; this is a town whose authorities believe it not a bad idea to protect with a cordon of police its Jewish exiles for the few days of return.

A short street connects the Allerheiligenplatz with the town's capacious central plaza, the Hauptplatz. The perimeter of the expanse is lined with old dwellings, two or three stories high, the shingled roofs at a sharp tilt to lighten the load of snow in heavy winters, ground-level shops fronting the sidewalk, stretches of which are shaded by Gothic arcades overgrown with ivy. The buildings damaged in the British and American air raids have been restored in the old style. We lived on the second floor of Number 11, across the Plätzl, an island of similar buildings clustered in the center of the plaza. The Plätzl's far side faces the Rathaus—the town hall—at the opposite edge of the square. On market days, the Hauptplatz's open expanse is thronged with horse-drawn wagons and carts of produce, meats and sausages, cheese, and baked goods, brought in by peasants from the nearby countryside, and with household wares, clothing, and all manner of goods conveyed by truck from Vienna and other cities. The Mariensäule towers in the middle of the main market sector. It is an elaborate construction of religious statuary encircling a column from which a figure of the Virgin Mary gazed over roofs and fields; the monument was erected in gratitude for her guardianship when the town was threatened by a visitation of the plague. I avoided the spot as a child, averse to approaching a shrine so impressively, compellingly, idolatrous. The Virgin is gone, demolished by Allied bombs; only her pedestal, the column, has prevailed.

Four avenues fan out from the Hauptplatz, in the directions of the four winds. At the entrance to the Neunkirchnerstrasse, close by the passage leading to the Allerheiligenplatz, there is another, almost unnoticeable relic of the early Jewish community. Chest high, a thick iron ring projects from the corner building's masonry. It is the anchor link of what was a chain that on Friday nights and Saturdays marked off a segment of the street to form an *eruv,* the symbolic circumscribing of a precinct that gives it the quality of a private domain, permitting observant Jews to carry things within its bounds and not transgress the laws of the Sabbath. Only Dr. Bastl knows the circlet's original function. In more recent times it has been used to tether horses.

Afternoon tea in small groups at the homes of our hosts. The warmth is ingenuous, almost childlike, and there suddenly comes to mind a different Christian posture to the Holocaust, a contrast that enables me, finally, to put my finger on what is unique about the Ichthys people. Years ago, I saw an article by a well-meaning Protestant minister that appeared in a Jewish periodical. It spoke eloquently of Christian guilt, and it made a demand: It was the Jews' obligation to forgive. Only then could the world be put right again. Sin, confession, forgiveness, grace. There was nothing in the formula that spoke of a perpetrator's accountability beyond admission. Only the victim's duty to absolve. I responded with fury. Let the parson, I wrote, shout his importunity over the wasteland of Babi Yar and the killing forests of Lithuania, let the bones and ashes contemplate his theology; living Jews cling to another theology, one in which action alone can bridge human conscience to divine remission; ours is a God of mercy, but *imitatio dei*—the imitation of God—is in the *doing* of His ways, justice and compassion. The Ichthys people talk a great deal about God—and they act, they seek unceasingly to follow. The logo on the week's program handed out to us is from Isaiah, "Comfort ye, comfort ye, My people, saith your God," and they have assumed the task of comforting.

We attend an evening meeting of Aktion Mitmensch, Wr. Neustadt's human rights association. The session is held in a conference room of St. Bernhard's, off the Neukloster's courtyard. A *kasher* buffet has been set out, the food ample and good. This is an odd venue for such a repast, it occurs to me: The saint was not known for a particular fondness of Christ's kinsmen. We sit with our servings at long tables, longitudinally arranged, that face a shorter one from which the Aktion's directorate presides. The people next to me have familiar names. They owned the grocery and delicatessen store to which my mother dragged hungry urchins off the streets for something to eat; the owners tell me they remember her stormy entrances.

The Aktion expresses its satisfaction at our coming, our return. It is a testimony to *Menschlichkeit*—humaneness—renascent in this town. Then the business part of the evening begins. Reports of shocking human rights violations in many parts of the world are read and discussed. Israeli "brutality" in the occupied West Bank and Gaza is an item on the agenda. I become uneasy. I have been a critic of many of my country's policies and actions. But when I hear accounts of Israeli offenses, echoes of distortion rebound; the accusations too often are undocumented, exaggerated, out of the context of confrontations in which they are said to have occurred. Israel is weighed against standards not imposed on its foes. That is, perhaps, as it should be; Jews have had the temerity to cry to the world that they are a light unto the nations. But not infrequently, antagonism toward Israel is confluent with animosity against Jews; anti-Semites have discovered in Israel an acceptable target for their venom. I am uneasy, yet I cannot doubt the sincerity of the people here tonight.

TUESDAY

Marianne Neuber: "How Can I Not Tell Them?"

Marianne Neuber has been one of the few to defy the ring of ostracism that seals Ichthys off from the polity of this town. She had heard of the plans for the *Woche der Begegnung,* called Helmuth Eiwen, and asked for the chance of a meeting between students of her school and our group.

She is Professor Marianne Neuber, the title signifying her position at the *Bundesrealgymnasium* in the Gröhrmühlgasse; her fields are history, psychology, and philosophy. Petite, blonde, attractive, she is in her mid-thirties. One's first impression is of a soft-spoken, reserved, almost shy young woman. But that impression quickly gives way to another. The easy graciousness is not a product of timidity. It seems, rather, to flow from a self-knowledge and self-assurance that are as resolute as they are modest. And there is something else that she projects and that I begin to grasp as I talk to her now, at 9 o'clock in the morning, waiting for the students to take their places in the assembly hall.

What brought her to arrange this encounter? I have been told by Helmuth that it was at her insistence, over the disapproval of most of her colleagues and with only the reluctant acquiescence, finally, of the school directorate. Is she drawn, religiously, to Ichthys?

No, she is not, she replies. She is Roman Catholic, she attends mass regularly.

What, then, prompted her to bring us to the school?

Her students must know their country, their history, she says. That cannot be without knowing what happened in Austria after March of 1938, what was done by Austrians here and in the armies of the Reich. The younger generation are unaware of a Jewish history in Wr. Neustadt. Most of them have never seen a Jew. They have been shielded from knowledge of the camps, the mass killings. She teaches her students what the Holocaust was. She cannot profess instruction in the social sciences and leave the vacuum of *Fürchterlichkeit*—of horror—undisturbed.

Is an introduction to the Holocaust included in the prescribed content of her courses? I want to know.

No, she laughs, the Ministry of Education hasn't come around to that yet. Then she frowns. But that shouldn't matter, should it, she asks in return, when something very important is being pushed aside? The *Woche* is a special opportunity. She has given this morning's program the title *"Zeitzeugen berichten"*—Witnesses to a time report. The young people should know at first hand, not only from her words and from the booklets of Holocaust history to which she subscribes.

Doesn't that cause her a great deal of trouble, taking liberties with the curriculum, and now becoming engaged with this agenda dreamed up by an excluded outfit?

She peers at me, perplexed, as if searching the question for meaning. They must know . . . how can I not tell them?

Another face raised to me in sudden astonishment swims into consciousness from out of the mind's repertoire of visual images. It is of an old Polish woman. She sat in a wheelchair in a reception room at Yad Vashem, in Jerusalem, the medal and certificate of her formal investiture into the ranks of the "Righteous Among the Nations" on her lap. As the Germans were evacuating Auschwitz before the advancing Russian troops, two young sisters slipped away in an unguarded moment from the S.S. death march to the west. Shaven, emaciated, in striped prison smocks, the girls ran through a patch of woods and, exhausted, beat on a farmhouse door and begged for refuge. Before the man who opened could collect himself, his wife, coming up from behind, grabbed the girls and rushed them into the cellar. She clothed and fed them until the Russians secured the area, a month later. Now she sat, old and frail and very much alert, at Yad Vashem. I bent over her and asked: Why? If the Germans had searched the farm, you and your family would have been shot! She looked at me, on her face the bewilderment of a polite person asked to respond to a nonquestion. But how could I not? she said.

Everyone has taken their place, a hundred and fifty or more students, sixteen- and seventeen-year-olds, our group in the forward rows. Fritzl Hacker, Walter David Riegler, and I are seated on a slightly raised dais. We three are the delegates of the witnesses. We are to unseal a time capsule, the life and death of Jewish Wr. Neustadt in the days of our youth, our flight, our thoughts on this reluctant return. The students will question and challenge. Marianne makes her request: The exchange should be uninhibited, no niceties, no masking of raw truths, only testimony and reflection.

This morning is to be the overriding justification—for me—of the return, so Helmuth Eiwen argued in his letters: If in memory lies salvation, then memory must be wielded as a tool for change. These young people might be shaken loose from the complacent disavowal of their elders. How good are the chances of planting memory's seeds in the Gröhrmühlgasse? I ask myself now.

The Gymnasium's director enters. A thin, stiff gentleman, he makes the correct introductory comments. He is authority *de jure,* but he is colorless, and his distancing from the moment seems to me evident. The authority in the field is, arrestingly, Marianne Neuber, the respect and affection in which she is held by the students palpable.

We speak our witness, the other former Wr. Neustädters occasionally adding theirs, amplifying. Again, as I listen to the others, I realize how temperate was the ordeal of my family's exit. We were no longer in Austria when the wave of fury was unleashed in the *Kristallnacht;* most of the others were. I did not lose parents or siblings, my grandmother survived Theresienstadt; the family trees of most of the others have close branches hacked off in the deportations and camps. Yet, there were deaths in my family that have left a hurt not scarred over. Aranka. Three times my age and a few years more when, still a preschooler, I crawled into her feather bed on icy winter mornings in Bratislava, finding warmth against the mysteriously resilient body, its immediacy accented by the thin, tousled shift, the sleepy cachet of her faintly olive-hued skin piercing the embrace's innocence . . . and innocence gave way to an awakening intimation of bliss. When she was married off to a dealer in eggs and poultry, a nice, square, plodding man of farm produce whom I remember vaguely as a foil to her slender, mischievous elegance, I felt abused. If I couldn't have her, I resolved, I would marry their daughter. But Erika, at the age of ten, disappeared together with her mother into a train of sealed cattle cars to the East. My sexuality has not been arrested at a girl's prepubescence; unlike Humbert Humbert, my first great love was kindled not by a Lolita but, rather, by the young woman who became her mother, and all the passion that has turmoiled in me has haloed, like an atom's penumbra of electrons, around the icon that was my cousin Aranka. I think of that now, at this moment's silent inventory of loss. Yes, mine has been more bounded. But, no, it has not been distant.

More than an hour passes. The delegates of the witnesses are finished. The stillness in the room has been absolute, uncanny because it is so unexpected. These are adolescents. One hears their schoolmates from other classes rampaging cheerily through the hallways outside during recess. But these in the assembly hall seem to have lost speech and movement. They sit upright, their attention fixed on the faces of the speakers. As if they, the *students,* were witnessing the unveiling of something from another planet, something so overwhelming that it robs them of speech and mobility.

In my report, I did not touch on my intended leitmotif of Jewish indestructibility. Here, that would have been ludicrously inapplicable, an incomprehensibility. One can throw down the gauntlet of defiant survival before an enemy who has threatened it, before a bystander who walked away sneering when it was in the balance. But these children . . . they have no more than a cloudy perception that once, a long time ago, before their time, Jews also were caught up in the disasters of war—in death, hunger, displacement—that ravaged Europe. But nothing that specific, nothing they could directly associate with the old people they were brought by their teacher to hear. Nothing that has touched them in depth. It has touched Marianne Neuber, who is not that very much older than they are. They admire her enough to have come along quietly and have quietly given us a hearing. And in this hour they have been made retrospective witnesses to an apocalypse. Laid out before them is an epic of suffering, selective, gratuitous, not a function of war itself and vastly more cruel than the clash of armies. They believe the composed cadences in which the saga of genocide has been recited before them.

What they have heard should suffice. The point has been made, they can no longer be unaware. But I am obsessed with words, with what, precisely, sharply, they are meant to bridge. Words are charged with too many shadings; I don't trust the accuracy of their vectors. When I hear them called out or see them transfixed on paper, I find myself enmeshed in threads of faceted meaning that spin from them and that so freely can enshroud them in ambiguity. Has their import been skewed by the imprecision of the speaker, the confined tuning of the hearer?

Perhaps the obsession devolves from the Jews' endless preoccupation with words, with the syllables and sentences of their canon.

> And a redeemer will come to Zion, and unto them that turn from transgression in Jacob, saith the Lord. And as for Me, this is My covenant with them, saith the Lord: My spirit that is upon thee, and My words which I have put in thy mouth, shall not depart out of thy mouth, nor out of the mouth of thy seed, nor out of the mouth of thy seed's seed, saith the Lord, from henceforth and for ever. . . . And You are holy, residing in the praises of Israel. . . .

Isaiah's template of salvation; a covenant of words.

I am troubled. Have we transmitted enough of a seed in this seminal hour? What will take root in the hearts and minds of these stunned, wide-eyed kids?

But the words have sufficed.

There is a pause. Several girls are dabbing at their eyes. One is sobbing, then she raises her hand and stands. The first question, only it is a statement, uncertain, tentative, not really a query:

"What was done to you . . . you can only feel hatred as you look at us!"

Several boys nod their agreement. A murmur of negation begins to unfurl from among the front rows but before it can coalesce into a response, several other students raise their hands.

"How can you *not* hate us?" A direct question.

"Now that you've come back, aren't you thinking 'We would have stayed here, had good lives, our friends would still be living, if it weren't for these people here'? Why do you want anything to do with us at all?" Another.

Fritzl Hacker and Walter David Riegler swerve their chairs slightly, toward me. It is the community's leader who should speak; the inquiry is to us all. But the Oberrabbiner lies in his Long Island grave, and I, too, am Weiss, and so, *in loco parentis,* words are mandated to me.

I think: The students have mirrored our own demurral when the Eiwens first approached us. A thread of synonymy between victims and perpetrators' blameless descendants! For me, certainly, hatred was at the core of reluctance. I have tried to keep before me the obligation to differentiate, contaminated crowd, unstained individual. Act on that, give benefit of doubt. Each human being a *tabula rasa* on which the person etches a record. Guilt of fathers not to be exacted from unknown sons. And yet, whenever—so unavoidably often—there has stared at me, blankly, still another portrait of their unfathomable brutality, I have fantasized: Could I, by pressing on a button, send them all, the German Volk and the Austrian, to the bottom of the sea, I would unhesitatingly press, and gradings and differentiation be damned.

But the fantasy of vengeance always frays. The world exists differently in the perception of each human being, the person an entire universe; a life destroyed, a world lost, a life saved, a world rescued. Retaliation of cosmic dimension has a corollary: Co-option of the cosmic barbarity suffered. The veneer of civilized behavior is very thin on the German soul. The overlay on the soul of the Jew is firmer; millennia of insistence on the precious fragility of the soul's bodily casing have made for a film less permeable to primordial tendencies to fratricide. Dream murder is a lightly shouldered exercise, like high-altitude bombing. It is when the target's faces are discerned that difficulties arise, even for many with only a diaphanous veneer.

I have now seen too many Austrian faces to indulge retrograde fantasies lightly. Hate these troubled children sitting before us, here, now?

There is only a moment's reflection.

Then I say, No, I do not hate you. You have done nothing to me, nothing to the others with whom I came. On the contrary, I admire your courage. What you have willingly heard is hard. It is an indictment, but not of your selves.

"Don't you want to hit out at the Österreicher who did this?" a tall, fair boy insists.

I would gladly smash the head of an S.S. man from the camps, if I had the strength for that, I answer. But you . . . No! I could see you dropping by for a bite at my home in Jerusalem. Perhaps one day you might.

I hear myself say that and, to my astonishment, realize that I mean it.

In the front rows, several of our group murmur assent.

The tall boy won't let it stand; he is still troubled: "But hatred is a powerful emotion, in all people," he argues, "and of all, you have a right to it! Aren't you denying?"

Sublimating might be a better way of putting it, I suggest. When we are not hurt . . . the hatred dissipates. The Jews could not have survived with long hatreds. We have had too much cause for it, we would have given up in bitterness. Letting hatred fade, turning to whatever is bright, that has been an adjustment for us, to keep going. We don't forget, and we must not, but we are not good at cherishing malevolence. Perhaps that also has something to do with our religion. We believe that human beings have a great potential for making the world better, and we always fall short. So we are always on the razor's edge, between the promise and the failure. We must forgive ourselves if we are to live with ourselves. Perhaps there is a spillover from ourselves to others. When there is decency, we leap to respond, we put the evil aside, open ourselves to a fresh start. Jews believe in the importance of the moment, the here and now; when that is right we believe that goodness will prevail . . . something like that. I know, this is a sermon; I wish I could have said that more simply; I am afraid I couldn't . . . you know, I am a professor!

The teenagers look at each other, nonplussed.

I add something: There *is* something that's come down to you. An obligation, specially yours, because you *are* Austrians. You must know what Austrians were capable of, and you must not forget. Otherwise it can happen again, to other people. You must never let anyone talk you into dismissing another person's *menschliche Würde*, their human dignity. All human beings have God's image stamped on them. Even people you don't like. Human dignity is at the heart of being human. Robbing that is the great offense against God and against man. And from there it is not so many steps to building death camps. Keep that before you. And . . . visit us in Israel.

Their looks and gestures signify acknowledgment.

Little more than a year later, an exchange of students is under way between Marianne Neuber's classes and a school in Bat Yam, near Tel Aviv.

I ask Marianne to join us at Friday night services and then for Sabbath dinner in the Corvinus ballroom. She can't. She is a single mother, she explains, and does not leave her year-old daughter in the evenings. But, yes, she would like to see me again; she will come to the Neukloster later in the week if I can manage a free hour. We set a time.

Noon. Official reception by the *Stadtgemeinde*—the municipality—at City Hall, led by Dr. Wittmann, the Socialist mayor. He is very young, a slight, good-looking man, almost boyish in appearance, informal, unpresumptous, and also, at first, ill at ease. The reception is at his initiative, over strong reservations by other members of the city council. That took courage. There had been threats on his life after he had the portrait of the Nazi period mayor taken down from the gallery. Felix Szolcsanyi had been outraged by the subterfuge of its removal—the ostensible need to replaster the hallway's facade—but in this town it was an act that required determination. Now, he hosts a group of expatriate Jews, and in so doing he forms a bridge to the shunned Ichthys congregation.

There is a particular awkwardness when Helmuth introduces me to him, understandably so. Dr. Wittmann wrote me nearly a year ago, shortly after Johannes Vrbecky, a family friend, had sought me out in Jerusalem. Alluding to his knowledge of the once Jewish community's contributions to the economic and intellectual life of Wr. Neustadt, and to its medieval renown as a center of Jewish scholarship, the mayor reflected *"Aus der heutigen Sicht bedauern wir die Vorkomnisse"*—from today's perspective we regret the circumstances—that led to the community's destruction upon the Anschluss. It was his sincere wish, he went on, not only to awaken memories of its existence but also to forge new ties. The municipality stood ready, he concluded his letter, to appoint a committee for this purpose; what was my reaction to his proposal? He would appreciate the opportunity of a discussion with me.

"From today's perspective, we regret the circumstances" . . . An in-

ternal revenue official's contrition for the decimal mistake in a tax as-
sessment. I felt sickened by the mindless banality, mentally composed a
harsh riposte, then finished reading the letter, and recalled Johannes
speaking highly of the man's liberalism and integrity. I stepped back.
In my reply I informed Dr. Wittmann of my "conflict of emotions"; that
I welcomed his idea, but a return to the streets that were empty of those
in whose midst I lived my early life would be too painful; that I did not
wish to reawaken memories of a destroyed childhood and irreplaceable
losses. My encouragement of his proposal would have to be from a
distance. When some months later I changed my mind and accepted the
Eiwens' call, I wrote again, confessing the vacillation and its causes, and
offering to meet with him. Now, we stand and exchange platitudes for a
few minutes, until he delivers his mayoral welcome.

The reception is followed by a luncheon, also hosted by the municipality, in the hall of what once had been a Baroque Period Carmelite
church and convent and that now serves as a venue for civic occasions.
The tables are assembled to make a square around the room's center. I
am seated between Johannes and a heavy, red-faced town officer. The
kasher meals in their styrofoam cartons are set out. Johannes offers a
benediction, then I, in the traditional Hebrew, "Blessed art thou, Lord
our God, King of the universe, who bringeth bread forth from the earth."
More speeches. The meal over, I am asked to recite grace, and I do so,
the long version, chanting the verses in my tuneless voice; the melody I
aim for is the traditional Ashkenazi rendition. All of our group know it,
they join in, helping, and the melody survives. I am not usually that
punctilious, rendering the blessing's full length after a weekday lunch,
but this is the way Wr. Neustadt's Oberrabbiner would have done it,
and, yes, it is a festive repast for us because we exist, even here. *Am
yisrael chai* . . . the House of Israel lives. I feel good. All of us who have
come back do: a very minor declaration, a passing assertion, but it is in
our language, for us to sing out in what half a century ago was turned
into a void, for our hosts to hear.

The afternoon is free. I am taken to tour the town's hospital. Modern,
spotless, gleaming. The comparison with Hadassah or Tel Hashomer
or Beilenson hospitals in Israel that flashes through my mind is decidedly unfavorable to Israel's leading medical centers. My escorts are physicians from the oncologic service. We talk shop. Most of them were

trained at the University of Vienna's medical school. When the conversation turns to the explosive developments this century in medicine, there is, once more, a palpable discomfiture, the unspoken awareness of a gap.

So many of the founders of modern medical science were German and Austrian Jews: Ehrlich, Warburg, Emden, Meyerhof, Krebs, Landsteiner, Loewi . . . the roster goes on and on, the list of Nobel laureates an order of magnitude above the proportion of Jews in the population. Until the Anschluss, Vienna was the world's mecca of medical distinction. By the end of March 1938, more than 150 of the 200 members of its faculty of medicine were sacked because of non-Aryan origins or marriage to Jews. Many managed to emigrate in the coming months, when the German "solution to the Jewish problem" still lay with expulsion rather than genocide; some died in the camps, some who could not find an open door, by their own hand.

Edzard Ernst is a non-Jewish physician born in Germany after the war; he occupied the faculty's Chair of Physical Medicine and Rehabilitation in the early 1990s. Recently, he wrote in the *Annals of Internal Medicine*:

> Little opposition was voiced by colleagues remaining in the Faculty; the whole action was carried out without major disturbances and was enthusiastically supported. . . . The vacant posts were quickly filled with persons, mostly from the lower ranks of the Faculty, known not for their medical expertise but for their political trustworthiness. . . . Among the atrocities directly related to the Faculty were experiments done on human prisoners in Dachau. . . . The experiments entailed the torture of many Jews. . . . Such atrocities were later "forgotten," "swept under the carpet," or justified by their wartime necessity. . . . After the end of the war, a law condemning the former Nazi physicians was anticipated but never materialized. . . . Of the two hundred teaching staff of the Faculty, only nineteen were thought not to be burdened by a Nazi past. Those Jewish physicians who had the courage to return after the war were given no help at all in restarting their lives. Official rehabilitation of the victims was marked predominantly by its nonexistence.

Ernst concluded with the observation that "a loss of this magnitude (nearly 80 percent of a faculty) is difficult to recover even within two or

three generations, and the presence of the 'old spirit'—making a university career on the basis of factors other than quality of work—must be
meaningful for many generations to come." The recollection is meaningful to me now as I talk with the doctors trained by those generations.
They are up-to-date in the field. The Vienna faculty is again competent,
and most of them have had postdoctoral training abroad. But they do
not seem to be the products of a great institution. Competent, yes, but I
do not find the intellectual sparkle, the uninhibited challenging of fact
and theory, that I have come to expect from house officers out of Harvard
or Stanford or Albert Einstein. In the coming days I am approached for
medical advice by former schoolmates and by people from the Ichthys
community; that would have been extraordinary before 1938 in a town
served by Vienna's graduates.

This afternoon, as we talk medicine and science, we step carefully
around the margins of a history for which they are not responsible but
which they have inherited, a sort of *danse macabre* in which the partners
agree to make believe that the background music is not played by a
death's-head fiddler. I make my references to that history, as I must, but
I don't push it. If I am combative at every turn this week, I tell myself, I
shall dissipate any impact, shall be discounted, regarded as too raw, too
unresponsively hostile a presence. Perhaps. But then, why not? Am I
retreating too much? I am tired.

Hillie and Yair arrive, picked up at the airport by an English-
speaking Ichthys couple, Americans who had joined the congregation.
They will stay close to my kids and help translate for them. The rest of
that afternoon, that evening, and during the coming days when I can
extricate myself, we walk the town, Hillie with his recording machine
and video camera. This is what he has come for, to trace the map of his
father's and grandfather's life in this place.

We cross the Domplatz—the sprawling plaza dominated by the Dom,
the cathedral church, at its center—two short blocks from our house on
the Hauptplatz. This place, too, was one from which I kept a distance
as a child. The Dom was badly damaged in the air raids; sections are
still enmeshed in spidery scaffolding. An elderly couple walks by, then
stops and looks at us. He is wearing Lederhosen—deer-leather shorts
burnished to a deep chestnut, held up by suspenders—and a soft, green
felt hat, game bird feathers clasped to the band by a silver buckle, the

Austrian male's paradigmatic accoutrement. The attire had come to be associated, long before the Anschluss, with the nationalistic posture of the Empire's German-speaking population, a partisan dress code which, with the rise of the Nazis, was often interchangeable with the khaki brown of the S.A. The man smiles, his face open and serious, and stretches his hand out to Yair. "How good to see Israelis in our town!" he offers, glancing at our colorfully embroidered knit *kippoth*. "My wife and I had a wonderful stay in your country. Everyone was so *freundlich*—so very friendly—and helpful. We have such respect for your people; *Lieber Gott*—dear Lord—what you are accomplishing! And everyone against you! We wish you well. . . . What brings you here?" I tell him. They are delighted. *"Wunderbar, wunderbar . . . you do have friends among us!"* the wife exclaims. He tips his hat, says *"Habe die Ehre,"* the old gentlemanly greeting—"I have the honor"—and they continue on their way, the woman waving back.

Before we return to the Corvinus, we have tea at the Neukloster with Johannes. My boys are fascinated by the library. Johannes takes out thick, leather-bound volumes that are larger than portfolios. Some are illuminated manuscripts. Atlases of the world's strange flora and fauna, early maps and charts of the oceans with fantastic depictions of sea monsters. Texts of theology in Greek and Latin, medieval High German, and Hebrew. Ancient Bibles, *T'nach*, the Septuagint, Jerome's Vulgate.

Yair knows the Talmudic commentaries, Johannes Buxtorf's *Biblical Concordance* of 1632, and the other frayed rabbinic tomes in the bookcase of my disorderly study at home, but only a few of those go back much further than the early 1700s. They were my father's, had been handed down from the generations before him, their colophons, by pen or press, a heraldry of scholarship mustered from the domains of the Hapsburg and Romanoff monarchies, from Venice and from Florence. They were shipped in wooden crates from Wr. Neustadt to Vienna, the Nazis ascribing them no worth, across Western Europe and the Atlantic to New York and, after his death, to northern California and then finally across other seas to Tel Aviv and up the winding road from the *shfelah*—the plain of the Sharon—to Jerusalem, the wandering Jews' inseparability from the Book. They were thumb-marked and annotated and invaded by book worms even before they began their long journey. The crates had not always stood up to the watery passages. I still read in them but they are worn and used, like the people who could not part with them.

The Neukloster's collection is more imposing, the Church's library, too, triumphant. Many of the volumes in the Cistercian *Bibliothek* are of far more venerable age. Their bindings of rich, tooled leather and the hasps and locks of silver that secure their mysteries from the unbidden eye seem to have withstood the attrition of centuries. They stand in massed ranks, row on row, covering the four walls from floor to ceiling. Standing in the center, beneath the distant ceiling's late Renaissance frescoes that are the only point of reference to a fixed moment in time, the viewer may feel his temporal moorings slipping, feel afloat in an amorphous, timeless dimension of thought and creativity, the sensation hallucinatory, not unlike that I have had in the oval chamber of the Orangerie, encompassed on all sides by Monet's water lilies and drawn into the confluent canvas, drawn down from the lucid present at the surface into unfathomed depths.

What is Hebrew doing here? Yair wonders. I race through an abridged commentary on the origins of Christianity and Western civilization and of how, in the Middle Ages, the monasteries were the repository of the world's fund of wisdom, but the talk is really extraneous to the moment. Yair is a *sabrah*—a native Israeli—and Hillie almost so, and they are not given to winged flights of the imagination. But they, too, are caught up in the richness of this gathered treasure of the mind's life, and they touch the books with an almost reverent gentleness.

Johannes accompanies us to the hotel. Before going in for supper, the boys and I stand before the tombstones in the wall. They try to decipher the inscriptions. A young man and woman are also there. Judging by their dress and the dialect of their speech, they are ordinary people, working Austrians. The girl is speaking with some intensity, pointing to the stones and explaining; he listens attentively. Shyness is not something Hillie has inherited from me. He walks up to the pair and asks her what it is that so engages her, that she is transmitting to her friend. I translate. Her reply is straightforward. She teaches in a school for severely handicapped children, some have cerebral palsy and other neurologic afflictions, some are retarded or emotionally disturbed. She believes it will help them to know they are not the only children excluded from a normal childhood, that other children have suffered more, the boys and girls of the persecuted Jews who were driven out from this place long ago and, again, in our times. Her handicapped pupils know help and compassion, the Jewish children knew only terror. The stones are a witness. She brings her class here and to the Eisenstadt museum of the absent Jews of the Burgenland so they may learn something of the inequality of pain. Before she can accept the young man's proposal of marriage, he must understand that, must understand her. She smiles, bids us farewell, and goes off with him, arm in arm and still in animated discourse.

An exhibition of paintings by Leon Abramowicz, a Jewish artist from Czernowitz who survived the war underground in France and until his death in 1973 worked in Vienna, opens tonight at the former Carmelite church. The exhibition was planned to coincide with our return. The rooms are crowded. The talk is of art and of Jews. Pissaro was also Jewish, announces an elderly lady who came from Vöslau to admire the oils and gouache washes; she seems very pleased to have remembered that. And Modigliani, and Soutine, weren't they Jews, too? a banker tries to recall. A few other names are put up for the roster of Jewish aesthetic achievement, and the chatter trickles into the quicksands of the ethnicity of European culture. Everyone is almost certain they can name at least one famous Jew, but then there were the Nüremberg Laws, a single Jewish grandparent conferred the privilege of membership in the tribe, and its disadvantages, and today one asks whether too broad an attributing of the membership aligns one with racism or philo-Semitism or something of both? Some of the non-Aryan greats had wished decidedly to forego the honor; Karl Landsteiner, a founder of immunology, had sued a publication for naming him in an article about the Jewish contributions to science and the humanities. The people here tonight are unquestionably at their generous best, but the ground they negotiate is tricky. Then someone mentions Isidore Kaufmann and David Kohn . . . ah, those were Jewish painters, unequivocally, their subjects were Jews, and everyone is on firm terrain again.

A slim, tall man in his late seventies introduces himself. He holds a sheaf of papers under his arm and stretches them toward me. "I am Flanner. I have some things that might interest you, and I want to tell you about your father." I learn later that Professor Karl Flanner is a historian. He is known as the *"Ideal-Kommunist,"* the idealistic communist. He was a member of the Communist Party, and he also has a reputation for having ignored its directives when they ran up against his ideals of humanity and kindness. The integrity had not impressed the Nazis. He spent much of the war in Dachau and Buchenwald. Now he writes articles about Wr. Neustadt's Jewish community. What he hands me are reprints of some of his essays.

"About your father," he begins. "When I was sixteen I was a *Lehrling*—an apprentice—in a carpenter's workshop, and I was sent one afternoon to do some repairs in the *Tempel*. No one was about, but then I noticed a light in the office. It was a winter day and already dusk, and a bearded man came out, the Oberrabbiner. Had I been to a synagogue before? he wanted to know. No, I said, and the rabbi asked if I might like to be shown around. I did. Then he offered me coffee and told me about the congregation and what went on in a synagogue. There was no condescension, only a straight conversation between two men, one still very young. I learned a bit about Judaism that day, and it has stuck. Your father was an unusual person." With that, he points to one of the papers he has handed me, the photocopy of a clipping from the town's newspaper, 1937, reporting my father's Yom Kippur sermon. My father invoked God's blessing on his congregation, the town and its *Bürgermeister*, and on the Nazis in Germany. . . . They, too, are God's children, and may He open their eyes to the errors of their ways. I did not know that speech, undoubtedly glad of the opportunity to sneak out when father's attention had to be on more important matters, and wilding about the courtyard with the other boys, proving my grown-up independence.

I notice a man my age waiting to interrupt the conversation.

"I am reluctant to approach you," he says when I turn to him. "There are people who say I am a Nazi, but I am not. You don't remember me? I am Friedl, I was your schoolmate!" He takes a photograph from the inner pocket of his jacket. A class picture, I am standing next to Herr Leposchitz, Friedl a row below me. I recognize myself, but not him. I don't remember him at all.

"My father was the *Bürgermeister*," he goes on. "They took him to Dachau." Karl Flanner nods, he knew that. "They took me, too," says Friedl, "a couple of years there and then other KZs in Germany. *Da war ich noch ein Junge*—still a teenager—and when the American doctors arrived they didn't think I'd make it."

Nazi. I can understand the aspersion. Anti-Semitism and National

Socialism coalesced this century. But anti-Semitism has been the age-old hostility, and not all its merchants have been as deadly. In his "Confessions of an Antisemite," Gregor von Rezzori paints a not entirely unfamiliar picture: a lady, his aristocratic grandmother who could not give the time of day to Jewish neighbors, yet, seeing from her windows Nazi rabble assaulting an old Jew a few days after the Anschluss, rushes to his defense, furled umbrella a weapon, and shouting, That is too much! Some of the German clergymen who protested against the Nazis' measures had anti-Semitic credentials. A few years ago I recommended, successfully, a Polish farmer for Yad Vashem's award to the Righteous Among the Nations. I had by chance met his granddaughter in Hawaii. She told me the story that had gone untold: He had sheltered Jews in occupied Poland throughout the war, provided for them, let loose his dogs to distract the S.S. squads when they came to search, refused gifts of money from his charges. He also belonged to a fascist, anti-Semitic Polish militia, but death factories . . . not that.

Friedl and I face each other. He is an alumnus of the same sojourns as some of us who returned, a graduate. Bürgermeister Zach was high up in the Christian Socialists, the Catholic clerical party. They were called "*die Schwarzen*"—the Blacks—for the Roman collars of the priests. Many of their leaders were eloquently anti-Semitic. The mayor was not known to be a great friend of the Jews, but my father, who had communal dealings with him, thought him, all considered, a moderate. The Nazis tolerated no competition from other groupings of the Right, hounded the recalcitrant into submission, some into the concentration camps. The camps and death can be an overarching connection. We shake hands.

How to put it all together? I am very tired.

Late that night Hillie is on the hotel's patio questioning the Wr. Neustädters who returned, his tape recorder in hand. They tell him stories about Schatzi, the Oberrabbiner and Frau Oberrabbiner, the community before 1938. I listen from the side; some of the stories are new to me.

Fritzl Hacker at sixteen had let it be known that he and some other progressive teenagers were forming a branch of the *Shomer Hatzair*. That was the far Left, defiantly antireligious Zionist movement. On New York's Lower East Side, I watched kids of their youth group on Yom

Kippur parading in front of synagogues, ham sandwiches in hand, and when I was a soldier in American-occupied Germany, the red hammer-and-sickle flag was raised above Zion's blue-and-white from flagpoles at their compounds in the displaced persons camps. Orthodox Jews regarded the *Shomer Hatzair* as offensive apostates. "Your grandfather," Fritzl says, "just smiled when he heard. 'All-right,' he said to me, 'but you are, just the same, a member of my congregation. I spoke at your bar mitzvah. We all love Zion. You want a branch of the *Shomer*? You can meet afternoons in the *beth midrash*—the *Tempel*'s adjacent study house—and if you invite me, I will come and speak to your club about our land.'"

WEDNESDAY

Landscape and Memory

Leaving the Neukloster after breakfast I pass Frau Piribauer at the kitchen's entrance, cradling a baby. The little girl has a rash on her arm. What does the professor from Israel think? I assure the mother of my ignorance in pediatrics and dermatology. Has the child been seen by a doctor? I inquire. She will take her later today but, nonetheless, what do I think? It looks like an innocuous allergic reaction. I have a mild cortisone ointment upstairs which I can give her if the physician advises and the stuff is expensive at the pharmacist's.

At the hotel, our group boards a chartered bus. We are joined by Helmuth and other Ichthys people for the trip into the Burgenland. The countryside is beautiful, a late spring day; the lonely clusters of white clouds accentuate the blue purity of the sky and intermittently stain the pale green fields and meadows with shadow. An unmarked sedan with five of our detective guardians precedes the bus. As we travel the secondary roads, little seems to have changed in the last sixty years. Fields and orchards and woods, here and there pheasants and rabbits at the edges, are interspersed with hamlets, the churches' steeples and onion domes sometimes the only indication of their presence in the landscape's hollows. I recognize many of the names on signposts at the crossroads. Landscape and memory.

First stop Eisenstadt, the Jewish museum. It is housed in the Hildesheimer *Bethaus*, the synagogue. Eisenstadt had been the pivot of the Seven Communities, the Hildesheimers for several generations among its noted families. Located in one wing of a courtyard on which other apartments open—gentile apartments—their home and the *Bethaus* had been spared Nazi torches. It was turned into a museum after the war. No Jews remain in the Burgenland. Our guide is a Catholic. I gather his is a nearly full-time position; classes of schoolchildren from throughout Niederösterreich are often brought here. Upkeep is provided by the Jewish communal organization in Vienna; I don't know whether the man has a salary, but it is clear as he explains the exhibits that he regards his trusteeship over the Jewish past as more than a job, as a vocation.

The vitrines display the gamut of ceremonial objects. There are some outstandingly crafted *Besomim Büchsen*, small decorative containers in silver or shaped wood, often a simulacrum of a medieval castle's turret, for holding cloves of cinnamon or other spices that are used in the *havdalah* ceremony at the Sabbath's ending, to escort with sweet fragrance the Queen's departure for the week. There are Torah scrolls in their velvet mantle, and a scroll of the Book of Esther that is read on Purim, the holiday commemorating the story of Gordian intrigue at the court of Ahasuerus, king of the Medes and Persians, that led to deliverance of the Jews from the hands of the evil Haman in the fifth or sixth century before the Common Era. The last words of Julius Streicher, the Nazi functionary whose crusade of pornographic anti-Semitism earned him a foremost standing in the hierarchy of genocide and a death sentence at the Nüremberg trials, were "the Jews have another *Purim!*"

As we leave, a swarm of ten-year-olds are ushered in with their teacher; the guide requests silence. Our group walks to the Jewish cemetery. Many of the weathered tombstones are only with difficulty discernible in the waist-high grass. We push it aside at several spots and recite the *kaddish* over graves without names.

Kobersdorf. Many of our group had settled in Wr. Neustadt from this village. All that is left to draw us back to this and the other places in the Burgenland, the still-intact anchors of memory that make the journey more than a sentimental passage through childhood's fading scenery, are the dead who have remained.

The cemetery stretches up a steep hillside where fields of grain and deciduous woodland edge the village. One could not from below know this to be a graveyard. There is no sign on the twisted iron gate, which cannot be pried open. We climb over breaks in the low, crumbling stone enclosure. The small building near the entrance, at which services were held before a burial, was demolished in the pogroms following the Kristallnacht; its shell has merged with the rich brush that clusters on the lower slope. Farther up, secondary forest has sprung from the densely fertile earth. The trees grow rapidly, their roots deep into the graves, undermining the stone markers which are sinking into the loosened loam or lying scattered on the surface under layers of fallen leaves and blackberry brambles. Paths have disappeared. We make our way holding on to branches, trying not to tread on hidden headstones or on the graves that are no longer marked. The roots and shifting mud have scattered their tiered ranks. It is difficult to locate a particular one. Uncertainties and assurances are whispered in the thickets as people separate into smaller groups and search: I am sure this is where *Grossvater* lies. . . . Are you, really? . . . I thought it was just above his parents, but there is nothing there. . . . I think, yes, there is. . . . And the old couple have found a lichened granite slab some inches down in the fragrant humus and are trying to right it with the leverage of a thick, dead branch. Several climb over to help, but we cannot steady it upright once it is lifted; we prop it at a low angle against an improvised cairn of gathered boulders. The chiseled letters on the surface have surrendered legibility to time and neglect but the grandson maintains he can make out a few words and an identifying mark: very faintly, interruptedly outlined, the palms of the *Kohen* held out above name and inscription, fingers splayed wide in the priestly blessing.

We are here a long time, forming a *minyan* again and again among the undergrowth and birches, a *kaddish* said for each of our dead, and if grave mounds or declivities can no longer be distinguished, that may not matter so much. This *is* the consecrated ground of the Jews of Kobersdorf and what is important is that the *kaddish* be proclaimed for every one we know here. The *kaddish* is not a prayer for the dead. It is an affirmation of faith by the living in the face of ultimate loss. *Yithgadal v'yithkadash shmeh rabbah, b'almah di vrah chiruteh v'yamlich malchuteh, b'chayechon u'v'yomechon u'v'chayeh d'chol beth yisrael.* . . . Exalted and sanctified be His great name in the world He created according to His will; may His kingdom reign in your lives and your days and in the lives of all the House of Israel. . . . The ancient Aramaic phrases bind the dead to the living in an endless presence.

It is past noon but we have one more stop to make in the Burgenland. Another village of the Seven Communities, another Jewish graveyard. Lackenbach. Robert Blum's people are buried there, and the father of Simchah Glaser, my friend in Jerusalem. Our convoy halts at the head of a hedge-lined lane. A very old, bent-over peasant woman is trimming a row of hawthorn. We are not sure this is the path, and we ask her. She barely looks up, does not care for the visitors and the interruption, and mumbles indistinctly, How should I know? We walk a few hundred feet and come to a high wall and gate, shut with a large lock. The cemetery lies on its other side, a flat field, high weeds coming to seed, but the tombstones can be made out. No way in here, but Robert remembers another entrance and walks back to the main road that curves into the hamlet. Someone points him to a house on its far side where a key is kept. *Kaddish.* I leave a stone, as I had promised, for Simchah's father, who was rabbi in Carynthia.

We pass through many villages of the Burgenland and Niederös-terreich on the return to town. The gabled, seemingly ageless cottages back on parcels of land, gardens and orchards and acres of ripening grain and bright yellow rape. The air is fragrant with lilac, white, pale purple, and deep crimson. Tulips are at their height, lilies-of-the-valley and peonies are coming out along the village greens at the foreground of the churches, many Baroque or older, that are the epicenter of each community. The villages are traversed by brooks and streams . . . the Laitha, the Fischa . . . I had caught minnows in those. Mallards and an occasional swan float on the waters which appear clean and fresh. Holy statues stand watch on the bridges and punctuate the rural routes and intersections. Patron saints and apostles, the crucified Nazarene and his unblemished mother, gaze unblinkingly at the traveler, bouquets of wilted flowers at the foot of the molded plaster and carved wood effigies, slats of rough timber slanting to a peak above in a pious allegory of protectiveness that affords the icon no shelter against the elements. Inns and restaurants, their terraces shaded by towering, dense chestnuts in variegated bloom, are the other intermittent landmark, the *Wirt*—the host—in white half-apron ready at the gateway beneath the establishment's escutcheon. The decked tables and the polished glasses shimmering with the light that breaks through between the branches beckon with promise. The local wines are very good, the meals, advertised in chalk on small blackboards, excellent.

It is all exquisite and removed and very peaceful. For us who once called this land home, it is also very empty.

Later this afternoon I am alone with Marianne Neuber in Pater Johannes's casually disordered office at the Neukloster, and the something else that she projects becomes evident: a simple, sweeping disbelief in the inevitability of human evil. She doesn't pronounce this, of course. She is unaffected, almost self-deprecating, so much so that I am painfully aware of the contrast with my own conceits. What she reveals of herself filters through indirectly, unintended, in response to my questions. Head tilted slightly, amused, skeptical, blue eyes steadily on me. Well, yes, there are not many among her colleagues who sympathize with her insistencies. . . . History must be presented unexpurgated of its unpleasantnesses, even when the truth hits home. . . . She is so preoccupied with what took place in Austria after the Anschluss because so few are. . . . Sure, it hasn't always been comfortable, sometimes there has been hostility.

Her bookshelves are not typical of an Austrian household. I learn that at the end of the week, when I stop by her flat with a farewell gift. What at once catches my eye is a volume, the *Black Book*, that traces from the beginning of recorded civilization to the present, in all their minute awfulness, the thick strands of cruelty that run uninterruptedly through the narrative of human doing. There is a collection of Holocaust writings, histories, survivors' memoirs, periodicals, their pages interspersed with inserted slips of paper that are marked with her annotations. Hers is not a lack of knowing, not denial, not a glossing over. She is well informed of evil's sway in human affairs. But she cannot accept, and she cannot desist.

Something is troubling her, something given away by her expression when she arrived at the monastery. I find out what it is only later, from someone else. She had just left a meeting of the Gymnasium's faculty council. A pupil faced dismissal from the school for a misdemeanor, the punishment harshly out of proportion to the infraction. She fought, a minority of one opposing the acquiescence of the others in the director's notions of discipline. In the end, her persuasiveness won, the sentence was reduced to a period of probation . . . and she was rebuked for once again—*schon wieder*—being stubbornly, disagreeably out on a limb for some cause. *Schon wieder* counsel of the underdog. It isn't the rebuke that bothers her, it is the incomprehensible want of heart and reason. Must you always take that on yourself, to defend? I ask her one day when I come to know her better. *Aber wieso denn nicht?*—but how can one otherwise?—she asks in return. It is a genuine perplexity. She is very innocent in her commitment, but also steely. We are not helplessly programmed to evil, she says, it can be resisted. She seems incapable of compromise on anything when compromise would be tacit acceptance of the unavoidability of a wrong. The nonconformism is not a posture; it is an unexpendable part of her, and I doubt she is aware of its intensity.

The hour allotted to me in the schedule dictated by Johannes and Helmuth is quickly over, but it has been enough for a bond to form. I accompany Marianne to the monastery's wrought-iron gate and stand there until the trim figure in the bright red suit disappears from sight. Then I admit to myself an awareness of still something else that she projects: charm, femininity.

Pater Dr. Bernard Springer arrives as Marianne leaves. He is priest at the Minorite convent's parish in Neunkirchen. I had heard about him before this week of return, and asked Johannes to arrange for a meeting. Dr. Springer took it on himself years ago to keep the Jewish cemetery in the town from decay; he personally tends to its upkeep. Neunkirchen was part of my father's community, and I wanted to express my appreciation. We walk in the Neukloster's meadow. Springer is a robust, good-looking man in young middle age. His easygoing manner bespeaks a spacious amicability and open-mindedness. He knows Jewish belief and history, and the short time we have together before my next appointment is crowded with warm, relaxed talk. He dismisses my words of respect for his guardianship of Neunkirchen's Jewish dead. . . . But that is obvious—*natürlich*—he says, how would I not? and changes the topic. I could easily become friends with this priest serving in a Franciscan order; like Johannes Vrbecky, he so contradicts the grim ancient pattern of unrelenting, tonsured enmity to my God and my people.

While I hold audience in the Neukloster, Hillie and Yair are on the trail of the phantom cat that sixty years ago crashed into my life. The pious tale of Mitzikatz has been told and retold in our *Sukkah* on the nights of the week-long Sukkoth autumn festival ever since Hillie was three, and the cat has grown in size and stature and ferocity with the decades. My sons continue the tradition with their children. In legend's permutating reaches, Mitzikatz, so black—*black!*—that chunks of anthracite beside him would pale to gray, feasts mostly on bulldogs. The beast's real-life progenitor had left on me an indelible impression and it appears the mark is now imprinted on my offspring and on theirs and will be for time without end an inseparable apocrypha of the holiday.

The *Sukkah* is a temporary hut, improvised under the open sky, its sides fashioned of boards or cloth attached to a wooden frame, its roofing made up sparsely of twigs or reeds so that the stars above can be seen. The Children of Israel are said to have sheltered in such fragile shanties during their wanderings in the wilderness; it is where, later in their land, they dwelled in the fields when autumn orchards and vineyards ripened for the harvesting; it is meant, too, as a reminder of the frailty and transience of man's existence on earth. The huts are gaily decorated, fruits and ornaments of colored paper hang by threads from the covering branches. The head of the household presents gifts and sweets. The *Sukkah* is to be lived in for a week, and even young children join the grown-ups spending the chilly nights on cots and sleeping bags. It is a great holiday.

There was no room to erect a *Sukkah* in the courtyard of our building on the Hauptplatz, and so we joined the Blum and Jaul families in theirs. The Blums and Jauls, cousins, owned a wholesale food supplies store in an alley off the Wienerstrasse. A capacious hut roofed with bulrushes was annually put together in the yard, up against the storehouse wall. Mina and my mother brought the meals from home a few streets away, struggling with vats of hot food stacked on notched aluminum grips.

The mythology of Mitzikatz unfolded on a brisk October evening, 1935. Everyone was dressed for services in the *Tempel* that opening night of the festival and for the opulent meal that awaited in the *Sukkah*. *Kiddush* and the occasion's special blessings were recited. My mother in her best silk dress placed an enormous—*enormous!*—bowl of chicken soup with *Knödel*—dumplings—before my father at the head of the table. The broth was boiling, as my children and grandchildren have been reliably informed, boiling as if it were a kettle of liquid steel flowing from the foundry's crucible, pillars of seething steam rising sacrificially through the bulrushes straight to heaven and obscuring my father's face as he bent over, spoon already lifted and blowing at the bubbling soupçon on its intended passage between beard and moustache. But at that very fateful moment, a tomcat was also on the prowl for its supper. The mice were scuttling on the *Sukkah*'s precariously smooth reeds, perhaps in flight from another feline patrolling the premises. The tom pounced, missed, the reeds parted, and the beast, black as hell, descended into my father's soup. With a piercing, Stygian shriek it leaped out and raced the length of the table into the nigrous night. My father, paralyzed for a fraction of a second, the spoon, now emptied, arrested in midair, white shirt and rabbinic frock bespattered, shouted into the shocked stillness *"Der soton hott a groisse gevureh"*—Satan has great powers these days—the only time I heard him in Yiddish, a tongue not his, until we came to New York's Lower East Side, as if the devilish apparition of the singed cat evoked memories of his days on the Galician front where that was the language of the impoverished Jews for whom, as in Isaac Bashevis Singer's fantasies, demons and dybbuks roamed the alleyways and imaginations of the *shtetl*.

It has fallen to me to tell and retell the story, as if the Weiss coat of arms were a howling cat rampant over crossed cattails, and the younger generation breathlessly awaits my rendition of the parboiled animal's screech. Over the years, that has grown in volume, in ear-splitting falsetto register. The neighbors in Berkeley and Jerusalem have come to know that no murder is at hand and they no longer call the police. But my children's skepticism has also grown. I have repeatedly sworn to the legend's veracity, but then, I also enjoy a family reputation for exaggeration and embellishment, and its telling, although insistently beseeched, has been heard as one might hear a particularly vivid exploit of the Baron von Münchhausen or an Amazon Indian's harrowing escape from mean-spirited ghostly ancestors in the forest. Until a few years ago. Then Edith Jaul, who with her siblings had wound up in Montevideo, paid us a visit in Jerusalem. A few years older than I, she had sat down the table from me the night of the beast. Yes, of course, she remembered! The cat was not really blacker than coal, and when I reproduced the shriek she thought she remembered it to have been a bit less agonized, but, yes, there was a cat in my father's soup and it had been a performance. Mitzikatz and I are vindicated, and now, guided by her cousin Robert Blum, my son and grandson undertake the *haj*—the pilgrimage—to the unforgotten site. The store is no longer there, of course, but there is the open yard, some cats are skulking about, and Yair, faith renewed, is persuaded of their pedigree from the one I had dubbed Mitzikatz.

Dinner at the Neukloster. The cook has made me potato latkes—a kind of thick, greasy pancake—and there are bowls of applesauce and sour cream. Latkes are the quintessential nourishment during Chanukah, when Jews brave oleaginous indigestibility to commemorate the finding of the little flask of pure oil with which to relight the candelabra in the ancient temple that had been desecrated by Seleucid armies. The oil, sufficient for one day, wondrously sufficed for seven, which fortunately just falls short of exceeding the outer limits of gastrointestinal tolerance. American Jewry has contributed the garnishing of dairy cream and grated apple. Scoffers maintain that latkes, a late European invention, are no more than a calorically apt fare for cold winter climates. Be that as it may, they are now associated widely with normative Judaism. (In the 1960s, a mixed cadre of California flower children camping out in the chaparral near Big Sur celebrated the Feast of Lights with latkes and rattlesnake steaks.) I am grateful to Mrs. Piribauer for the kindness.

The meal is hurried because Johannes and I must move on to the *Sparkassensaal* for the *Dichterlesung*—poetry recital—by Elazar Ben-Yoetz.

The *Sparkassensaal* is an auditorium on the second floor of a building that had its beginnings in the mid-seventeenth century, as a Jesuit college. The edifice has changed hands several times over the past three centuries, has been in secular hands since 1798, and eventually was given over to a savings and loan institution, a *Sparkasse*. It seems that churches and convents in this Catholic town not rarely undergo a metamorphosis of mission, from godliness to banality, as if the two arms of authority of what had been the Holy Roman Empire—the sacred and the secular—remain bewilderingly intertwined, a perpetual convenience for the managers of society. In earlier periods, witches and heretics and Jews were shifted from the grip of the one to the other as the stages of accusation, interrogation, dungeon, and torture progressed to stake and gallows. With the rise of consumerism in modern society, the very sanctuaries of the old apostolic faith are shifting occupancy, giving way to accommodate the creed of possession. It's none of my business, of course, and I am short on pain for Rome, but I have a moment of bemusement reflecting on the transmutation of Ignatius of Loyola's fervent precincts.

Elazar Ben-Yoetz writes poetry; he will read selections from his opus at 8 o'clock this evening. He is the youngest among us who returned; he was an infant when his parents fled after the Anschluss. German continued to be spoken in the home. Ben-Yoetz works in several languages, but German is the metier of his muse.

Dr. Wittmann and the municipality are once again our hosts. The hall is festive. There are several hundred people, moving about, chatting in small, commingling groups, balancing half-empty glasses of wine. Some of the ladies are in evening dress. Wr. Neustadt's society is present in strength, and I perceive no hint of anything out of the ordinary as Ichthys and establishment mingle. Dr. Wittmann is relaxed and charming, as if he has grown accustomed to the strangeness of this week and its company. He introduces me to the notables gathered around him. One is a stately gentleman whose name I recognize. Hans Barwitzius is one of the contributors to *Finis Austriae,* an anthology of reminiscences by Austrian opponents of the Nazis who lived through the days leading up to and following March 11, 1938. He was active in the Social Democrat movement which, after 1934, was outlawed by the right-wing regimes of Dollfuss and Schuschnigg; its underground leaders tried, unsuccessfully, to persuade the government to armed resistance as German troops stood poised to enter. After the war, Barwitzius was one of Dr. Wittmann's Socialist predecessors in the mayor's seat. Our conversation is easy, no gymnastics around uncomfortable historical handicaps. Another man I could come to like.

I am less comfortable in the exchanges with some of the others who approach me, older people. There is a repetitive theme to the intelligence they seem pressed to share with me—the acquaintance with cherished Jews who disappeared after Austria became a province of the Third Reich: Doctor Strauss who came on his bicycle nights when the baby's whooping cough was out of control and asked no money because he knew the unemployed father had none; the storekeeper who extended credit for month after month when there was plain hunger in the workers' quarters and who didn't pursue the accounts; a neighbor who cared for the children when the mother was in hospital. It isn't that I question the sincerity of the storytellers this evening. They are not bracketing their affections and regrets with accounts of their own wartime miseries. No one introduces a contrapuntal motif, real or ludicrous. The score of such compositions I know well, from my army service in Germany, from the talk of Austrian and German visitors in American living rooms: "The war was terrible . . . so much suffering . . . the bombings . . . the racial laws against the Jews . . . I remember when there was so little to eat, ja! and we ate horse flesh! . . ." Nor are they figuring causalities: "What happened to the Jews cannot be excused, surely not. . . . But one must understand what brought the Nazis to such extremes . . . the unemployment. . . . Did you know, more than half the doctors . . . the lawyers . . . the professors . . . were Jewish?" Disharmonies of episode and statistics pitched at an equilibration of woe. There is nothing like that tonight. But neither is there spoken aloud just to what destinations the missing Jews were disappeared, just what was done with them there.

What should be my response to these unfinished commiserations?

I appreciate their feelings. Then I revert to my ground theme, the program I set myself on returning: See, we were gone, we disappeared, but we are still here. Jews have been for the burning, but not the Jewish people. We are phoenix, we are salamander, we come through flames.

These are very nice men and women, the people who will listen to Ben-Yoetz, and I modulate the defiance. But it hangs in the air between us.

I have always detested stand-up parties and receptions. Glasses or plastic cups from which *en gros* wine or indifferent gin swilling around an expired onion gradually evaporates into the cacophony of babbled politesse, grasped in precarious apposition with the hand-outs of fast food and nonabsorbent little napkins; facial contours in a rictus of sustained merriment as meaningless one-liners borrowed from a thin thesaurus of banalities are parried. I feel my self's inner space encircled and violated by unknown bodies, the muscles of my legs tensing for escape. Since a battalion of surgeons general determined secondary inhalation of tobacco smoke to be dangerous, there is not even the preoccupation with pipe and matches to lend a moment's pause for introversion, nor the analgesic blue-gray haze to screen from the barrage of social inanities. I normally don't last very long. Clutching a handkerchief to staunch the sudden attack of coryza or waving a hand in the direction of an imaginary friend at the far end of the room, I break out, find refuge in a lavatory or in the stolen company of a non-lionized guest with whom a conversation might be essayed.

But such escape is not an option for me in Wr. Neustadt. I am here flying a flag. I am the spokesman for an extinguished community. The colors cannot be abandoned. So I feign a sudden interest in making the acquaintance of an elderly gentleman at rest on a nearby divan, excuse myself, seat myself next to him. A minute later, a good-looking lady takes the place on my other side, her presence undeniable. She co-opts my chat with the gentleman, there is room on the divan but she is pressed close against me; immaculately décolleté and perfumed, she mentions a little corner cafe near where she lives, later this evening or the next we might have a quiet drink there. In another place, a young-er woman's unexpected coquetry would lend élan to an occasion of programmed conventionalities. But this is a place where shadows and images of the past crowd the present. They need no recovering. They are there, instant associations with a phrase heard, a feeling registered. *"Ich bin eine Judendirne"*—I am a Jew's whore—read the signs hung on the chest of Aryan women paraded by S.A. through German and Austri-an streets, women who loved a Jew, women who had only bantered with one at a party. That was *Rassenschande,* a shameful sullying of Ger-man purity. It is very ungracious to my attractive companion of the last minutes, but light flirtation cannot bear the weight of ghostly meta-phors, and I change the topic to benign comparisons, the weather, the heat this May in Niederösterreich, veritably a breath out of the Arabi-an desert.

The reading is about to begin. Folding chairs have been set up for the audience. Ben-Yoetz sits on the podium, behind a small table on which his books and manuscripts are arrayed. His appearance is magisterial with his salt-and-pepper beard and the expansive black skullcap he has donned, bringing brow and pale face into dramatic relief. His voice carries, he articulates each word, slowly, with gravity. What Ben-Yoetz is declaiming bears the tonalities of a great profundity. "He is just like one of the ancient Hebrew prophets," the man next to me murmurs to his wife. She whispers back, "Yes, just like a Doré print of Jeremiah or Ezekiel." The simile is in order, I think: The voice resounds but there is no hearing. His prose is ornately convoluted, the idioms thundering upon each other, flowing into a rococo symphony that is marvelously incomprehensible. The Austrians are dazed, awed, but we Israelis, prod-ucts of a less tactfully refined cultural milieu, look at each other, What in heaven's name does the man want? I never really discover that. In my best Viennese manner I congratulate his performance at its close and gingerly seek clarification of the more arcane passages. Ben-Yoetz only smiles, generously.

But there is something else this evening that, on the face of it, is

joyously understandable. Klezmers! During intermissions in the reading, a trio plays music, *"jiddisch/chassidisch"* music, the program notes
have it. A fiddle, a guitar, an accordion. Young men. They call themselves *"10 Saiten–1 Bogen"*—Ten Strings, One Bow—but their names are
not announced. They accompany the instruments with song, in the *hei-
mish*—the familiar, homey—Yiddish dialect of Poland and Galicia, and
they are very good. As I sway to the melodies I wonder, however did
these folk musicians from a world that is no longer find their way to, of
all places, this gentile town?

When they are finished, the fiddler introduces himself. Herwig
Strobl. I am jolted from my reverie. Decidedly not a Jewish name. Neither are those of the other two, Ivo Truhlar, Günter Wagner. As he begins
to speak, Strobl is clearly aware that we are perplexed.

"My father would not be pleased with me tonight," he says. "My
father is buried near here. He was a Nazi, an important man in the Party.
When I turned sixteen, I pledged myself to preserving what he wished
to destroy. I became a musician, and I learned Yiddish. So have my
companions. They are not Jewish, either. We cannot bring the dead to
life, but their spirit, yes, that is in their songs, we sing for them . . . a
reminder . . . there is fire in the ashes . . . maybe another beginning. . . .
Good night."

After they leave, I find a stack of pamphlets about the group. They
have given concerts all over Europe, and in Canada; performed in theater productions of Jewish themes; led workshops on Jewish thought
and culture. They have set motifs from Chagall's paintings, Paul Cel-
an's poetry, Agnon's fiction, to arrangements of Jewish tunes—Yiddish,
Sephardic, Yemenite, Israeli.

I *talk* memory. Strobl and his friends render it in sound that resonates
far deeper than can speech, in the chords of the heart.

The formal program over, the remainder of the evening is to be at
leisure, socializing with Wr. Neustadt people. Around the buffet tables—
the food *kasher*, no longer a surprise this week—there is elbow room;
instead of the barbaric cocktail hour's juggling one can rest plate and
glass on counters, and the interchanges are not so vapid.

A man my age tells me warmly that we were schoolmates, four years
in the same grades at the *Übungsschule*. He has a class picture, there I am
at one end of a line of pupils, he at the other. Much as I try, hard as I
search his face and my memory for shreds of familiarity, I can call up
nothing of a recognition.

In the following days there will be other such blank, bewildering failures of recall. Yet, the few Jewish children in the faded school photographs I know well, know what they were, how we related, ordinary small occurrences. And the Jewish kids from other classes and other schools, from the *Tempel*, fidgeting together during youth services *Shabbath* afternoons, from the allées of the Stadtpark and Akademie. But the gentile boys and girls who now come up to me, aging men and women, reminiscing of some commonality . . . the only one I can think of at all is Max Stiglbauer's brother Rudi whom I pushed over in his *Hitler Jugend* uniform. Was I that shut off from the world of children who were not members of the tribe, even before the Nazis swarmed in the town? Was the bivalency of my growing years that pronounced, the line between what could not be forgotten and what was not to be remembered that sharply drawn?

The schoolmate's wife is here, too. They must talk with me. We find a quiet corner. She had cancer surgery a few months back, they are terrified of what may come next. . . . Is the treatment she is undergoing the best that can be? Are the local physicians knowledgeable? Once the doctors here were good—she doesn't say "the Jewish doctors," but I think that is in their minds as well as in mine. May she give me a copy of the medical records, would I advise her? Yes, of course I will. I will discuss her situation with an oncologist in New York.

Before turning in at the Neukloster I stop at the Corvinus to check for messages. The detectives at the entrance and in the lobby give me a nod of recognition.

THURSDAY

A Day with Ichthys; The Wings of the Dove

This is the big day for Ichthys. We shall spend the hours from late morning to late afternoon with the congregation in their house of prayer. Our program brochure describes the order of the day as a *Festversammlung im Gemeindezentrum der Ichthys Gemeinde,* a festive assembly in the Ichthys community center. "Church" and "service" are not mentioned. Yet Ichthys makes itself known as a *Freikirche,* a free church; they do not as a rule circumlocute their ecclesiastic identity. Their pick of words today is a finesse: They know that nowadays many Jews, even committed Jews, feel free to be present at the ceremonies and worship of other religions—as silent, respectful bystanders; they also know that what we cannot do is participate.

I reflect on this as our friends usher us into the building.

This day with Ichthys is to be a sharing of experience. Aspiration to transcendence is, more than anything else, what distinguishes man from beast, all men whose inner hearing is not deafened. We Jews can come together with all human beings to affirm the common impulse, to enter the dimension of spirit that coexists with our materiality. Where we do not follow is in the routes and rites of the passage. To accompany others there would be to erase meaning and value from our conceptions. Not only our customs and guidelines but the core of our covenant differ, have uniqueness. And the obligations we have taken on ourselves. Parallel lines perhaps meet in the infinity of the Absolute. But the dimension in which we exist, here, now, is infinitely variegated. To compress lines of seeking into a uniform strand does violence to the soul's sanctum of self, of individuality. It is man and God who search for each other, not humanity and godliness. The quest is sacred, the brotherhood of man holy if there is a God who is holy. We do not merge paths; we do not trade our passports, not our cards of identity. But encounters with other travelers, a relating of the journey's acquired wisdom, surely yes.

The encounter now to begin in the *Gemeindezentrum* of Ichthys is special. Not only because they reach out so passionately to the Jewish people, but also because the passion of their faith stirs a responsiveness. I am attuned to other rhythms in analogous space. They can evoke new vibrancies in the ones to which I move. If I were to choose the proverbial single piece of music to have on a desert island, it would be Beethoven's *Missa Solemnis*. The *Missa* holds for me an unrivaled majesty. I persuaded the girl who became my wife to a first date by the offer of a Sunday morning at St. Patrick's Cathedral in New York; she had not before heard High Mass sung. Years later, we stayed with friends of the Institut Pasteur in Paris during winter vacation. Christmas Eve there was a party. My wife and I were the only Jews in the crowd, and we were the only ones who left early, for Notre Dame where for a thousand years the birth of the savior of the gentiles has been commemorated at midnight. Be in Paris and let that pass me by? I thought. The other young biologists thought otherwise: A commitment to science does not go well with metaphysical appreciation. For me that appreciation is unconfined. Prominent in my early collection of records is the series of

Ethnic Folkways field recordings: The ecstasies of an Inuit shaman or a Sioux medicine man's totemic chant, the raw, unpostured yearnings of unsophisticated peoples living close to earth and sky speak powerfully to me.

The *Freikirche*'s hall of assembly is a long, unadorned room. The high, plain cross on the raised platform at the far end has been nearly obscured by a banner of fabric draped over the crossbeams; the embroidered letters spell the prophecy that Ichthys has taken for its communiqué to the Jews: "Comfort ye, comfort ye . . ." The room is filled with chairs and benches aligned along tables covered with white linen.

There are many speeches, interspersed with communal singing. We are given song sheets so we can join in. The verses are from Judaism's elemental profession, the *Sh'ma*—"Hear, O, Israel, the Lord our God, the Lord is One"—from the Psalms, from other passages of *T'nach*, the Hebrew Bible. We are together with Ichthys in hymns of praise, of God's glory and of His chosen people Israel, hymns that could as well be in the repertoire of a synagogue's cantorial evening.

The congregation's boys and girls dance on the platform, accompanied by piano and accordion. The Eiwens' older children lead the group. Dances and music are mostly Israeli and, judging by the smooth flow of the choreography, they have been well rehearsed. Streamers of crepe paper in blue and white are twirled by the dancers and at the closing of the performance are linked to form a huge Star of David stretched above their heads. They end with a loud "Shalom!," and present each of us with a rose—a Rose of Sharon, one of the adults reflects. We are astounded. The skill of their act, the children's grace and graciousness, are startling. Delighted with themselves, the youngsters smile and laugh and wave their hands. "Shalom, shalom," they repeat.

The welcoming remarks by Helmuth and Uli are very earnest. They explain, once again, that it is God's work, not theirs, that has brought us here. It is God's hand that directs every step they take. He has opened their eyes, guided them to their Christian duty: To dedicate themselves to His service they must dedicate their hearts and souls and means to work for the Jewish people, their love of God must be confluent with their love of the nation with whom He sealed His covenant at Sinai.

There is nothing in what they are saying now that they have not said already, eloquently, persuasively, when we met in Jerusalem and in their many letters. What stands out today more than ever is the concentration, the power of conviction that pervades each sentence, every gesture, and the unabashed proximity with which they relate to the godhead.

Hillie, next to me, squirms. He is a deeply religious young man but he is ill at ease with the uninterrupted God talk. So am I.

We Jews, too, feel an intimacy with God. We express the sense of closeness in our prayers, in our small talk and our quotidian dealings. We address Him as *avinu malkenu,* our father, our king. Many of us preface and conclude a written memo, a spoken promise or intent, no matter how trivial, with the habitual pietism "Be it with heaven's help." And we petition Him, insistently, to live up to His attributes which we are charged to imitate. Our forefather took liberty with the Lord at the beginning of the acquaintance, holding Him to His declared essence —justice—in driving a hard bargain for the lives of Sodom and Gomorrah's perverse inhabitants. A few thousand years down the road, the hasidic master Yitzchak Levi of Berditchev subpoenaed the Almighty to a *beth din*—a court of law—in the *shtetl,* to justify the sorrows and disasters that befall the world, His dominion.

The relationship has been unceasingly disputatious, a sharp, reciprocal calling to account, and it has been of a ubiquitous immediacy. But no less ubiquitous is the counterbalancing of reserve, of trepidation. For all the dialogue of love and contentiousness, God for the Jews is ineffability. That may be strange, but it is so: intimacy with the ineffable. When pushed to the wall for His credentials, the Lord of the Universe would grant His appointed steward, Moses, no more than a cryptogram, "I am that I am." Our God of Abraham, Isaac, and Jacob dwells in the mists of Israel's praises, at once achingly near and inaccessible to the mind. The tension has kept us oscillating, dancing; it seems to have kept us spry.

Ichthys, I think, tilts the equilibrium. The reserve is stretched thin. In believing themselves inseparably interlocked with God, do they not trespass on sacred ground? Is that for some devout Christians a Christian unavoidability? The God of Ichthys is not only the unapprehensible God of the Patriarchs. He is also the Son, incarnate in Jesus of Nazareth, God both awesome and human. That is a mystery to Christians, a meaninglessness to Jews. There is anthropomorphism in every

language of faith: His outstretched hand, the seeing eye, king, master
. . . But for Jews the forms of diction do not encroach on that which cannot be held in words. We do not pronounce His name, do not grasp Him,
can only search. When others aver too great a knowing, I am disturbed.

Their fusion with the godhead's will, of which Ichthys is so passionately and touchingly convinced, leads to another intuitive divergence,
the authorship of commitment.

We Jews have taken a partnership in the perfection of creation. The
irreducible sacrament for us is action, action in the cause, and man's
freedom to choose and do is constitutional. Heaven's cause on earth is
given into mortal hands. We do not see ourselves as passive agents of
His will. We arrogate, rather, a temerity, we insist on an autonomy of
volition. God's will shall come to be done on earth, some day, somehow, by an anastomoses of pulses, His, man's. May we be spinners of
His web . . . , yes, by our understanding of the design, free artisans, not
contract labor on the assembly line. God's ways can be followed only in
the way of compassion for his creatures. The Talmud is astounded by
the biblical command to walk after Him—how can man so obey, seeing
He is flame? Shall we not be consumed? Even Moses, the faithful ser-
vant at home in the corridors of His dwelling, who speaks with Him
panim el panim—face to face—stands back from the burning bush! The
command is to assume His cause, the Talmud answers; as He calls on the
sick, so must we; as He comforts mourners, as He clothes the naked, as
He . . . as He trembles in care over mankind, so must we. We. Ourselves.
By our opting for the partnership. We all stood at Sinai and as one cried
into the seen thunder of the mountain *"na'asseh v'nishmah,"* we shall do,
we shall do, then we shall listen.

Ichthys no less serves God by reaching out in solicitude to the afflicted. They, as we, are convinced of the salience of deed at the inter-
face of God and man. Their commitment is fervent, extraordinary. Yet in
their avowed inseparability from heaven, the supreme value Judaism
assigns to the individual and his initiatives is qualified. The working
relationship they posit seems to me one between master artist and un-
derstudy, rather than of partners freely come to join an imperative venture.

Morning intermission. I am introduced to special guests. One is a
Pentecostal minister from Kansas, come all the way for this event. An

outgoing, enthusiastic man, inspired by what Ichthys has brought about, he intends to propose to his church back home a new reaching out to American Jews. Like the Eiwens, he dismisses attempts at mission to the Jews; there is no theological justification for this. And like the Ichthys people, his references to God are to Him who revealed himself to Abraham and his descendants. As I write, the Southern Baptist convention of the United States is launching a new campaign to "bring the Jews to Christ." Well, there has been progress at least with some Christian groups: Some have come to an armistice—peace?—with the legitimacy of our covenant.

Another visitor is a familiar presence in the congregation. A tall, bearded man in early middle age, dressed in slacks and open white shirt, crucifix pendent on the wide chest, Father Franz is also a Cistercian, and he is another maverick. An activist in social causes, he founded *Beth Shalom,* the House of Peace, a retreat center in a nearby town. His quiet bearing, eyes steadily on the person with whom he is engaged, the low, measured voice, communicate an unforced authority. This is a monk, I think after a brief conversation, whose vows do not include conformism. From what Johannes Vrbecky intimates later in the week, Father Franz walks on the margins of toleration by the order. I cannot but feel that I have met another Austrian priest it would be worth knowing better.

Several of our group take the lectern. They recite their stories of Wr. Neustadt, of flight, rebuilt lives, and the difficult decision to this reluctant return. Then I must speak.

I speak of the Torah, the Law. In the narrow, specific sense, "Torah" is the Pentateuch, the first five books of Scripture; in the broader sense, the term embraces the whole vast body of Jewish religious learning. The quintessential message of the Torah—the noun is in the feminine— is expressed in the aphorism, "All her ways are pleasance, and all her paths peace." The aphorism expresses a point of departure throughout Jewish jurisprudence: Where a statute or decree does not meet a given moment's concern for peace and compassion, the rabbis may suspend the specific rule. The principle overrides. It is sovereign over the affairs of all mankind, Jew and gentile.

I begin my words with this fundamental of Judaism because I wish to show that we see God's grace hovering over all his creatures. We and you, I say to Helmut and Uli and Ichthys, strive in different tracks but under the same auspices. I become extravagant—in the throes of my own rhetoric—and I give prominence to a rabbinic apothegm, a *midrash*: "I call heaven and earth to witness that whether it be Gentile or Israelite, man or woman, slave or handmaid, according to the deeds which he does, so will the Holy Spirit rest on him." An Australian aborigine, I insist, who lives kindly with his folk, attuned to the songlines of his land, is no less a cherished child of God than we assembled here today.

When they respond after I step down, Uli and Helmuth are troubled. Especially Uli. They do not reject my *midrash*, but its note is for them somewhat off-key. In so panoramic an ecumenicism, the Lord who revealed himself to the Patriarchs recedes in focus. The aborigine is too far removed, spiritually, certainly in genealogy, from Abraham's offspring. Again I wonder. Just where are the lines of salvation drawn for the Eiwens? Jesus was a Jew, but the religion that bears his name is not Judaic. Are its far-flung converts—Greeks and Romans, Celts, Teutons and Slavs, Africans and Asians, and Ichthys and, yes, the surviving aborigines of Australia who these days gather on Sundays in buildings topped by a cross—are all those magically of closer kin to the tribes of Israel than the peoples who have not heard his gospel or have let it wash over them untouched? That makes sense, in its way, for a Christianity that is aggressively missionary. But Ichthys disavows a Christian mission to the Jews. Only to the Jews!? That must be it, then! Only two covenantal bonds, the one with the God who spoke to Abraham and Moses, the other with the one incarnate in the Nazarene Jew and his church. Perhaps this is the differential between us: We Jews are bound to our revelation and our Law, and we also believe in the equality before the Master of the Universe of all who live by the moral code of the children of Noah, a parochialism tenaciously sustained side by side with an unwavering universality. Nothing novel, I reflect, in the observation, but it is in the encounter with this extraordinary, outreaching Christian congregation that my Jewish understanding takes on a sharpness.

The program continues after buffet lunch. We present the Ichthys community with a large menorah fashioned by Yemenite silversmiths in a Tel Aviv outskirt. A dedication ceremony. Leo Blum reads a text of our gratitude. The menorah is placed on the podium, next to a small oil lamp from the Byzantine period with a palm branch and cross in relief on its upper rim that is my personal gift.

Then I must speak again, to tell the story of the wings of the dove. The story was published years ago and I had told it to Helmuth and Uli one night in Israel. It happened in 1965 when I was in the Soviet Union searching to penetrate the mist of oppression and fear for moments of closeness with Jews. And the story has to do with what catapulted me into the land of Abraham, Isaac, and Jacob; that is why I am requested to tell it again now.

It was in Sukhumi, in Abkhazia, where the tumor immunology workshop was held, an exotic conclave of a few dozen Soviet and foreign scientists and a nearly equal number of Soviet intelligence officers who hovered about intimating to their citizens, many of them Jewish, the wisdom of keeping this unaccustomed interaction with the West coolly professional. I was constantly declarative of my Jewishness and there were fleeting, electric confidences exchanged with the Jews among the Soviet researchers—a Hebrew sentence clumsily scrawled between lines of data in my notebook, a tap on the knee by the professor recently rehabilitated from a Siberian camp and a sentence whispered as I bent down to help retrieve the napkin he let drop under the dinner table, "Be careful . . . we are frightened . . . don't believe anything they tell you. . . ." Persuasive introductions to a modern European version of Jewish reality.

I knew there was a Jewish community in Sukhumi, but the clerks at the hotel claimed to be uninformed of any synagogue or communal organization. It was from a passerby that I finally learned of a dilapidated building at the far end of town where Jews met. I went there late on my first day, at the time when the afternoon and evening prayers are read, *minchah* and *maariv,* the daily services which, according to tradition, were instituted by Isaac and Jacob. I arrived early. There was no sign identifying the place, and I knocked on several doors up and down the poor street before a door opened. Several older men were sitting in a dimly lit room, looking into Hebrew books or talking. Dead silence as I walked in. A tall, bearded man asked what I wished. I introduced myself, I am an observant Jew, a scientist, invited to a medical conference. The men, all Grusinian—Georgian—Jews, spoke among themselves before the elder again turned to me. As a young man he had studied at a *Chabad yeshivah* in Lithuania and he spoke Yiddish, the language of my own *yeshivah* education in New York. He was the *chacham* —literally, the "wise man," the rabbi. During the next half hour the conversation was stilted. I had no sense of welcome, rather that of a cautious questioning. No Jewish tourist had turned up for many years. Really, why had I, when surely the proceedings at the Beria *dacha* would take all my attention. My Yiddish was heavily accentuated by German —how did I come by that? Did I know how to pray? How did I locate this old building, once a manufacturing plant? Who told me about it? My questions, in turn, were carefully weighed, causing more talk among them in a Georgian language, and were then deflected. There were a number of Jews in town, yes, mostly Georgians like themselves, a few Ashkenazim. They were, of course, loyal citizens, everything was well with them.

More men arrived, slowly filling the room. Many of them wore the elaborately embroidered Georgian skullcaps common also among the general population. As groups straggled in, the *chacham* said a few words to each which I sensed to be an admonition: There was a nodding in my direction when I offered *"Shalom!,"* but no one really greeted me. The men, I was told, had finished the day's work at the town farm— the *kolkhoz*—where they do their share as good Soviet citizens—again! —for Soviet agriculture.

We entered a larger room, sparsely furnished as a synagogue, for *minchah*. The liturgy differs somewhat from the Ashkenazi but its core, the psalms and the standing *amidah*—the eighteen benedictions that were already statutory in the early Talmudic era—are identical. I declined the frayed prayer book handed me; I know the services by heart, and I recited the responsive passages loudly. That seemed to evoke surprise, but the reserve remained.

The concluding prayer of every service is the *olenuh*. It, too, goes back to the Men of the Great Synagogue whose students made the Talmud. "We bend and prostrate ourselves before the King of Kings . . . there is no other. . . ." The *olenuh* and the *shmah* are the flamed, almost fiercely compressed outcries of faith with which for some two thousand years Jews have died rather than betray. When we were done, I asked the hour of next morning's *shacharith* worship; that was instituted by the first of the Patriarchs. It is very early, shortly after five, before work; very uncomfortable for you, surely, the *chacham* was quite insistent, and there is always a *minyan*, the required quorum, you need not think you should come. He wanted to look away, but I held his eyes and said "I rarely miss *shacharith*. You don't understand!"

As I was about to leave, a thin, middle-aged man rushed into the room. He was unshaven, his clothes ragged. An Ashkenazi, he spoke Russian and Yiddish. He had just wound up in Sukhumi, truck drivers gave him lifts, over many days, from somewhere in the East. He was making his way back to near the Polish border where they had arrested him five years ago, he wasn't sure why, he was just let go from the Gulag, no money, no food the last two days. . . . He needed to spill all that out, but the men wouldn't let him. The *chacham* said: "Don't tell us. Don't tell us anything. We don't want to know. We will help you, you must go on. Now." He went to a small strongbox hidden behind a loose brick in the wall, took out the notes in it—there were at least fifty rubles, a lot of money—and pressed it into the man's hand. The beggar was escorted out by several men, not roughly but firmly. The *chacham* looked at me. "*You* don't understand," he said. But I did.

A quarter past five next morning. There were more than fifty men in the prayer room. Out of a community of only a few hundred families—as I later learned—that is an astounding number for a weekday morning; few orthodox congregations in America match that. I had my *tefillin* with me, mini-*tefillin* that my father had given me for travel. Wrapped in the velveteen bag adorned with a Star of David, they fit into the palm of my hand. The once black leather straps had turned a mottled gray, faded with use. The *tallith*—the prayer shawl—in my briefcase also showed the signs of wear, the white woolen fabric yellowed, the sequined silver collar—taken from my father's *tallith* after he died—tarnished. As I removed shawl and phylacteries from their covers there was a virtual transformation in the group similarly engaged around me: I had presented my ambassadorial credentials. I was surrounded, hugged, embraced. We were Jews together in a bad place, the recognition of generic covenant and state overwhelming. Laughing and crying and so many questions. Is it true what the papers and radio are saying about Israel? Do they know in America what is happening with us in this country? And, again and again, questions about Menachem Mendel Schneerson, the revered Rebbe of the *Chabad-Lubavich hasidim*. Is he well? And Rabbi L., who some forty years ago had been with them, the Rebbe's emissary, and had to flee to the States when the authorities cracked down harder on Jewish religious activism—how is he??

I learned that this community's only significant link with the Jewish world outside was the *Chabad* movement which managed to maintain a tenuous, thinly stretched web of communication with the villages and towns of the southeastern Soviet provinces. Yes, there were the Israelis from the Moscow embassy, they were seen once in a rare while dining on the hotel's verandah, but the Grusinian Jews were solidly traditional, those in Sukhumi displayed little evidence of modern sophistication, and they were not sure what to make of the Israelis and their breakfast of bacon and eggs. I was for real, I belonged with them.

I was at the prayer house daily, morning and evening, for the week of my stay. That was why I had come. Other than for my searching out fugitive instants of Jewish kinship with colleagues at the conference, science and research could be damned for the duration.

Friday night. Several hundred people at prayers, men, women, children. Only one or two were Ashkenazim. I was told that quite a number of families from the cities of White Russia had for years been living in Sukhumi, but they were not observant, and at any rate had buckled under the steady throttling of Jewish expression. The Grusinians had not, that was obvious. The service concluded, I was seated on a small wooden bench in the courtyard. There was little light, and I could make out only dimly the dense circle that formed around me. It was very quiet. I sat there for over an hour. Every few minutes one or several men and women stepped up, touched me, and returned to the perimeter. Not many words were spoken. Then one woman said through her tears, "When you get back, tell them we can't hold out much longer." A man called out, in Hebrew, "We must get back home, to *Eretz Yisrael.*" I could only think of the old rallying cry of the Diaspora, "Next year in Jerusalem," and when I pronounced that, so foolish a hope, there was a chorus of voices, "No, no, that's too long!" I wondered if all these people could be Sukhumi residents. As if he read the thought the *chacham* whispered "They have come from many towns in Georgia. You are important. You link."

Yes, very important, more so than at any other hour of my life. I thought of the mysterious figure, Eldad the Danite, who appeared in the ghettos of medieval towns in the West from the far side of the river Sambatyon with tidings of the lost Ten Tribes. That night it was in Abkhazia and the chain was forged by an immunology professor from the distant regions of San Francisco Bay. When we broke up, a man invited me home for *Shabbath* dinner. From the way he spoke and from what I already knew of the dangers such a home visit entailed for the host, it was an invitation that took courage. Others stopped him: No, too much of a risk, and to me, You shouldn't accept, you do understand, we all want you, but. . . . Two robust men in their decorative *kippoth* accompanied me back to the hotel. At the entrance they halted, stood for a few seconds square and solid in the middle of the road, and called out very loudly "Shalom, shalom," peace be with you. They retained their pride, these Grusinian Jews who around the turn of the century had come down from remote mountain settlements with a name for combative independence.

The last morning of my week in Sukhumi. The parting from the congregation after *shacharith* was tearful. "I shall be back. Soon as I can. We'll see each other again," I promised, always finding it hard to pronounce an emotional leave-taking's finality. The *chacham* was less given to fancy: "I wonder if we shall. Everything is uncertain. We've been stubborn, they say, pushing things too far. There have been threats. I'm not sure how far they will go." He asked if I could arrange for *etrogim* —*etrogim* from Israel—to be sent to them in the fall. The *etrog* is a citrus fruit related to the lemon. It is held in one's hand together with a palm shoot and branches of willow and myrtle during prayers on the Sukkoth holiday; the four species signify fruitfulness in the land of milk and honey where the earth is thirsty and water a commodity yearly to be beseeched from heaven. That I promised with greater confidence. Then there was a more immediate request. I had come that morning without my briefcase, carrying in my hand the *teffillin* in their starred pouch. Would I wrap that up in a piece of brown paper? The police could not be uninformed of the stranger's daily presence, surely, but no need to be conspicuous this last time on my way out! We held each other and I left, brown parcel in hand.

(I could not then know just how empty my promise of a reunion would prove to be. Two years later, the morning after the Six Day war broke out between Israel and the Arab states, the *chacham* and another elder were taken away by unidentified men in an unmarked sedan. They were found next day, hanging from a tree in the Jewish cemetery.)

It was still only half-light in the persistent drizzle and fog as I started on the unpaved road to town. I was the only one about. Then, suddenly, a gendarme appeared from a side alley. With a look of surprise and, it seemed to me, suspicion, he stopped me. What am I doing?

Taking a walk, I replied. The exchange was in a mix of languages—I had learned a bit of Russian, he had a minute vocabulary of English and German. No, he shot back brusquely, the suspiciousness more at the surface, American tourists no walk here . . . very far . . . no pleasure . . . so early . . . rain. Then, roughly, What you have there? pointing to my clutched right fist. I had a sensation of displacement in time and yet of a deep, ancient familiarity. This isn't new to me at all, flashed through my mind. A sense of déjà vu, like when one drives through a mountainous region never traveled before and as the highway curves the sunlit valley below comes into view, one knows it is seen for the first time and yet it is plainly, wholly known. A few weeks before I was bar mitzvah in New York, my father was showing me how, after prayer, to plait the thongs around the square leather boxes of the *tefillin* in which the handwritten parchments of the *sh'mah* are enclosed. The thongs should be wound to resemble the wings of a dove, he explained, because of Elisha, the master of the wings, and because the House of Israel is likened to a dove fluttering for refuge before the hawk. That comes from the Talmud:

> Rabbi Jannai said: "*Tefillin* demand a pure body, like Elisha, the Master of the Wings." Why is he called the Master of the Wings? Because the evil Roman government decreed against Israel that whoever donned *tefillin* would have his brains pierced through; yet Elisha put them on and went out into the streets. A quaestor saw him. Elisha fled before him. The quaestor gave pursuit. As he overtook him, Elisha removed the *tefillin* from his head and held them hidden in his hand. "What is in your hand?" the Roman demanded. "The wings of a dove," was his reply. He stretched out his hands and lo!, they were the wings of a dove. Therefore he is called Elisha the Master of the Wings. And why the wings of a dove rather than of other birds? Because the Congregation of Israel is likened to a dove. . . . Just as a dove is protected by its wings, when tired resting on the one and flying with the other, so is Israel protected by the Law.

And in this muddy lane on the outskirts of a small town on the shores of the Black Sea, the confrontation was very much the same. I myself was in no danger. There was no law in the Soviet Union forbidding a visitor to have *tefillin,* and if that were after all to fall under the rubric of hooliganism, I had the VIP status to back me up. But . . . I had just left a group of obdurate Jews who would not cast off their particularity, they were anxious to draw no attention to themselves, I belonged to the Cold War enemy and was making a nuisance of myself with the other, despised identity, the Jewish one . . . and the cop was hostile. Who are you? Why are you here? What are you keeping to yourself? he demanded. The age-old challenge. Without thinking, I blurted out the words of Elisha, in Hebrew: "*Kanfeh yonah*—the wings of a dove." The gendarme stared at me. Then he took two or three steps backward, turned sharply, and with rapid strides disappeared into the alley. I had no idea what terminated the interrogation just as it began. When I entered the lobby of the hotel I asked myself, Did this really happen? although I knew it had. I felt confused, slipped from my anchorage in time as it is parceled out by the clocks of Berkeley and Sukhumi and the protocols of cancer research, and firmly transposed into Jewish time.

In my mail slot there was the telegram from the colleague in Rehovoth inviting me to lecture at the Weizmann. I wired acceptance. Other segments of Jewish time in other Soviet cities and then the El-Al night flight from Vienna to Ben-Gurion airport outside Tel Aviv. *Shacharith* over the Mediterranean, off the coast of Israel. *Tefillin*. Very tired. Making my way through the raucous disorder of immigration and customs, I erred into the wrong corridor. A young policeman, waving his hands, stopped me. "That's not the right passage, Mister, you can't enter here!" he shouted. A senior officer a few feet away heard him, saw my bewilderment, clearly that of a weary newcomer, and glanced at the pouch with the stitched *Magen David* that I still had in my hand. He came over, a broad, swarthy man with a huge handlebar moustache, laughed encouragingly, and patting me heavily on the shoulder boomed at the other constable in the inflection I later learned to recognize as that of the Jews from North Africa. "What are you saying, this isn't the right way? Can't you see? *Hayehudi hazeh*—this Jew—is coming home on the wings of the dove! All ways into *Eretz Yisrael* are right for him." Then to me: "*Bruchim ha'baim!*"—welcome to the comer, and with that I was propelled into Israel. Circle closed. All the rest was detail.

That is the story of *kanfeh yonah* Helmuth and Uli wanted to hear again and I was glad of the opportunity. But language, in the final analysis, is alien to the sentiments it articulates, Joseph Brodsky wrote. I had to tell the Austrians something of Jewish continuity, not a pious homily but rather something of a stripped-down, stark piety from the Jew's quotidian book of hours and millennia. The story of the wings spans only the more recent two but I had found myself knitted into the strands and it would do.

Why has the continuity stood against all comers? I ask rhetorically. Neither sword nor fire nor prussic acid could extinguish it—See, here I stand, here we sit. I answer myself, and them, with the classical exegesis: The Pharaoh said to the Egyptians, "Come, let us outsmart *him*" . . . when he spoke of the Jewish tribes in their midst. Why "him" when he referred to a multitude? He should have said "them"! Because, the rabbis hold, Pharaoh's war was against the God of the people. It is against Him that the eternal enmity has always been directed. Because His hand is eternally on the Jews, shaking, demanding that they cry out their threat into unlit wastelands, "There *can* be light!" For as long as there are among them seven thousand knees that will not bend to Baal, God is on the line with them. Battles can be won against Him, but not wars. So we continue. "In your blood shalt thou live, in your blood shalt thou live," the prophet heard Him—even in your blood. That is the pledge. And we, we must forever choose light, even when the nations choose the dark rites of Thanatos. The Law is a law of life, its ways luminous. So we continue, in a bright rush of living.

My talk—a sermon, really, I am afraid—finished, there is a surprise. Carola Tengler, an attractive artist from the nearby town of Pitten who some years ago had joined the Ichthys community, has made me a gift: a mosaic of small tiles, set into a square of fired clay, in the shape of a dove's wings outstretched over the Hebrew letters spelling *"kanfeh yonah."* It is beautifully done, very much like the mosaic design of the zodiac on the floor of the Byzantine synagogue of Beth Alpha in the Valley of Jezreel and the other floor mosaics in ancient synagogues scattered over the Judean hills and the Galilee. It will lie on my desk at home in Jerusalem, a reminder of the dove's strange flights through space and time.

FRIDAY

Seven Centuries, Four Generations—Welcome, the Sabbath, the Queen

Vienna. We are taken by bus, less than an hour's drive from Wr. Neustadt. In the inner city we alight and continue on foot. It is just as I recall from childhood, wide tree-lined boulevards giving way to winding, cobbled passages and secluded squares that have changed little since their medieval layout, palatial residences of the old Empire's nobility and royalty interspersed with edifices of church and state and with gabled dwellings crimped and cambered, all crowded in a mosaic of style—Gothic, Baroque, Neo-Classic—that under the weight of years has taken on an aura of homogeneity. Near the fountain in the Graben I recognize the confectioner's shop where on special occasions Tante Hermine had brought me for a wicked treat, a round dark chocolate filled with candied cherry and liqueur. A Montessori kindergarden teacher of liberal leanings ahead of her time, she believed that the rare drop of alcoholic indulgence provided a happy counterpoint to the lovingly strict discipline she imposed on her pupils and young nephews and nieces. I was awed by her and very fond of her, for the bonbons and for the deep, warm eyes and no-nonsense firmness that somehow went together. From her the nod of approval meant something, more than the parental reward of a shilling every time I came home from school with a *römischen Einser,* the Roman letter 'I' awarded for distinguished achievement in the multiplication table or the spelling of the provinces' capitals. Not long after the last chocolate cherry, Hermine Nassau and her sister Helene disappeared into a train bound for Auschwitz.

My son and grandson are dazzled by the city's splendor. Yair has not been to a European city before, Hillie only briefly when he was nine as the family stopped in London and Paris on our way to the first experiment of living in Israel. They want to wander leisurely, to see and photograph, and they must have the *Eis* which, glorious and unique in all the world, can be attained only from a cart on the Schwedenplatz. The cart stands there, yes, exactly where I remember it to have stood on a spring day in 1936 as good and evil struggled for my soul. I had been permitted a day's outing to Vienna with the Reiningers. Willie, a year older than I, and Kurti, younger by two or three, were variously the comrades and bane of my youth. Their father, Hugo, *rosh ha'kahal*— the president—of my father's congregation, and mother, Veronika, a strikingly elegant lady of aristocratic manner, had persuaded my parents to let me join the expedition. But I had had a sore throat the week before, cold drink and ice could lead to a dangerous relapse, pneumonia or worse—the common folk wisdom of that time—and I had been pledged to refrain. The malaga sherbet of the Italian vendor was famous, and there I stood, torn between pledge and pleasure; the angel triumphed, and I managed a crestfallen *"Danke, aber nein"*—thank you, but no. If the way to heaven is paved with unconsumed raisin-flavored ice cream cones, the way to scientific medicine was paved, in my case, by want bred of superstition. Now, here, finally, the chance of a belated, vicarious apotheosis. But, once more, no. This time the adversary is not the angel Raphael, God's medicinal viceroy; it is our security detachment. The detectives are nervous. We must not stray. We must remain together as a group, under their eyes. With *kippoth* on the heads of some of us we are clearly a group of Jews, there are throngs of people milling about the Old City, and . . . the security men have their responsibility . . .

We walk briskly to the main synagogue, the *Seitenstettengasse Tempel*. My father had been wooed to take the rabbinate there shortly before the Anschluss. Had he accepted, it occurs to me, we would have lived in the metropolis; we would not have felt as vulnerable as did the Jews scattered in the provinces; he might not have felt the urgency to quit the country, and I would not be here today.

And the Reiningers? . . . Hugo was among the first from our town to be sent to Dachau. There he was sadistically abused and beaten until his release after some months. Damaged, stripped of everything he owned—they were a proud, wealthy family—he used the last of his means for visas and passage to Montevideo and a new life of pressing poverty.

The Chief Rabbi receives us in the sanctuary. He gives an overview of Jewish life in Austria today. The talk is prosaic, there is no verve, no spirit, but then I wonder if my impression is fair: Inevitably, I make comparison with my father when I hear a rabbi speak, and my father was a master. But the sense of mediocrity as I now listen to this one becomes stronger when he invites comments. Several of our group who have family in the cemeteries of the Seven Communities express dismay at their state of neglect—why is nothing done about that? The rabbi is bland. Improvements have already begun, he claims—we who have just been to recite *kaddish* in Kobersdorf look at each other—and more will hopefully become possible, but of course money is short, there must be priorities, there is the thorny question of who is responsible, the central communal organization or the regional Austrian authorities. . . . A prominent Viennese Jew who apparently has nurtured a quarrel with the communal leadership rises to launch a lengthy attack on the rabbi. Funds are amply available, he insists, there is a record of waste and misappropriation. Voices are raised, the meeting deteriorates into an exchange of accusation and counteraccusation. Whatever the authority vested in him, the rabbi seems incapable of exercising it. It is one of us returnees who calls for decorum. This is an affront, he says, the loud angry voices before the ark where the scrolls of the Torah are held. We all feel that. Communal divisiveness, failure of leadership. . . . I have seen this before, in American synagogues on the verge of dissolution, where the neighborhood has changed, the membership draining into the suburbs, and the sense of purpose dissolving in factional bitterness as if the energy once channeled to growth has, like an autoimmune reaction, turned inward against itself. This community here has not yet achieved a purpose, it has not yet extricated itself from the shambles of the Holocaust. Surely, I cannot blame. But I am ashamed, and I am embarrassed before the Eiwens and the other Ichthys people who have come with us.

We proceed to the *Landhaus,* in the Herrengasse. The *Landhaus* is the seat of the regional government of Niederösterreich. There is a reception for us sponsored by the parliament's speaker, but he is abroad and will be represented by a deputy.

We are received in the lavishly Baroque marble hall where committees of the *Landtag*—the House of Representatives—and the ministries meet.

"Herrengasse" . . . the word rings a bell. After some effort, it clicks: That was often my father's destination when he went to Vienna. And then it comes back. This is where sessions of the Ministry of Education took place; he was a member, inspector for religious instruction, compulsory in Austria's high schools. I mention that to one of our *Landtag* hosts. He smiles: "Perhaps you will be sitting in the chair that was occupied by the Oberrabbiner." There is a venerable Jewish custom not to usurp a parent's chair. That is regarded an impiety, even long after their decease. But all this week I've been so much my father's alter ego! As I take my place I once again have the sense of time eerily telescoping.

The speaker's deputy is an impressive woman. She minces no words as she offers her greetings at the luncheon—*kasher*—that follows the reception. It is of importance to her and to the House that we are here, she says. The nation bears a guilt before God and man that is unforgivable. The barbarous past cannot be redeemed, she will not pain us with platitudes of regret. She can only vow her determination to work for an Austria that will not again defile itself.

She has been deputized but clearly she is also speaking for herself. "Deputy" . . . Hochhuth's "Deputy" leaps to mind, an associative pairing. But this one addressing us now is very different from the one of Christ who reigned from St. Peter's throne in Olympian indifference while Christian nations ravaged the Jews of Europe.

A bus tour of Vienna's points of interest has been planned for the afternoon, but Hillie wants to get back to Wr. Neustadt. He has not seen enough of the town, he still needs to validate the geography of his father's sketchy tales. Could we take a train or bus back while the others tour the capital? I, too, would prefer a few hours of freedom, to confirm some of my memories. We consult in English, the language that remains in our family when personal matters are the topic. Dr. Schebesta, the *Landtag's* chief of protocol, overhears and puts his Mercedes-Benz and driver at our disposal. We race back on the new Autostrasse and continue stalking the past in the streets and parks of Wr. Neustadt.

FRIDAY NIGHT

Sabbath eve service on the stretch of lawn along the town wall where the Jewish tombstones are set in a row.

A path leading into the Stadtpark separates the lawn from the Corvinus. The hotel has provided folding chairs aligned three deep in a semicircle facing the stones. Our group is seated. Several hundred guests stand closely packed behind us. They are the Ichthys people and others from the town and satellite villages who have heard of the event and want to participate. Fathers Johannes, Franz, and Bernhard Springer have also come. There are newspaper and TV reporters, and, of course, our friends from security. Tonight there are many more of them. The path has been closed at each end of the site. Uniformed police with dogs patrol the area and people must identify themselves before they are allowed past the temporary barriers.

The service is to begin at 7 o'clock. I am to explain it and to say something about the significance of the Sabbath. Yair will then lead the first part of the liturgy, Hillie the concluding portion.

A microphone has been placed close to the wall so that our voices will be clearly audible, but Hillie doesn't like that. He is very punctilious in his observance of the day of rest which begins at sundown. It is not only toil but also acts of creativity and change that are enjoined. As *He* paused on the seventh day, so must we. We cease to intervene in the order of things, step back and float, wholly at peace, in time come to a stop. Fire and spark, more than anything else, are the epitomes of creative energy, and even the closing or breaking of a current should be avoided. I tend to be more casual than my son where the Law trickles into deltas of detail. Some rabbis, I point out, have ruled voice amplification permissible; this is a special occasion; and the sun is still high. Hillie is tense and will have none of it. He models himself more on the grandfather whose name he carries than on his father. "Your dad would not have played games," Hillie insists, and pushes the mike aside. I am not convinced of my father's inflexibility were he here this evening, but I am proud of this son.

I rise to speak, and the words won't come. How to draw coherence from the repertoire of images and thought that crowd my mind in glittering riot? So much that can be said, so much that must be said. At whom do I aim? At the people of Ichthys and the others waiting silently, reverently, to join in the Sabbath with us? Some of them have put on *kippoth,* brought by the caterer from Vienna, others handkerchiefs, like nonobservant Jews who on finding themselves at a religious event show their respect for tradition. One of Helmuth's congregants holds a Jewish prayer book, ready to join—he has been taking Hebrew lessons and can read some of the text. But in the half-moon row of chairs before me sit *my* people, for whom I am this week my charismatic father's surrogate—should I aim at them?

Make the minutes count!

So I take refuge in forthrightness. I am confused and frightened, I admit, the moment and the place are overwhelming. There is a sanctum . . . the Sabbath is sacred . . .

And suddenly it is clear, the uncertainty gone: This evening *we* are the hosts, my son and grandson and I and the Jews who have returned and the dead whose presence is engraved in the weathered tablets behind. I shall make the Sabbath as I do at home: Before the meal we exchange *divre torah* and *inyane d'yomo*—reflections on the week's Torah reading and its timeliness to day and season. Often, non-Jewish guests are at table with us. Hillel the Elder said to the gentile who wanted to know, "Go, learn!" We describe, we interpret. But we are wholly ourselves this night, Jews. We lift the cup of wine in celebration of the commandments *we* have chosen to shoulder. The Sabbath is remembrance of our exodus from the land of Egypt, we say in the benediction. Remembrance of slavery and redemption. Not only then. The Sabbath is our reprieve from bondage to matter and to transience. And in recalling the particular we imprint into our being, flesh and soul, the saga of oppression and liberation that is all mankind's. Remember me and guard me well, the Sabbath cries to the Jew, lest you forget the heaviness of shackles, yours and all men's, lest you take lightly the freedom that is all men's hard-won right.

That is what I try to say now about the Sabbath, for ourselves and to the Austrians.

I translate the passage with which the service opens, every evening service, the Ordinary of Jewish worship.

> Blessed art thou . . . who at thy word bringest on the evening twilight, with wisdom openest the gates of the heavens, and with understanding changest times and variest seasons, and arrangest the stars in their watches in the sky, according to thy will. Thou createst day and night; thou rollest away the light from before the darkness, and the darkness from before the light; thou makest the day to pass and the night to approach, thou dividest the day from the night, the Lord of hosts is thy name; a God living and enduring for ever, mayest thou reign over us for ever and ever. Blessed art thou, O Lord, who bringest on the evening twilight.

We recognize Him first as Lord of the wondrous cosmos and of all the inhabitants of earth. That is faith's foundation for the Jew: The universal. In the next passage, ". . . with everlasting love thou hast loved the House of Israel, thy people; Torah and commandments hast thou taught us . . . ," we acknowledge Him Lord of Israel: The particular. Only then can He be addressed, *My* God: The individual.

The universal foremost. Great. But I am standing on ground where not long ago the near-universal longing of the populace was for a golden age "when Jewish blood shall spurt from knife. . . ." That memory, too, wells up, and I shift. Today's Torah reading is the first chapter of Numbers. Moses is taking count of the tribes of Israel wandering in the desert—how many are there, how many have survived? *Inyane d'yomo . . .* I call out that question now, as dusk begins to settle on this bloody land. Ten of the twelve tribes did not come back from Assyrian captivity. Of the remaining two, large numbers were lost in Babylonia, so many more to Hellenistic cohorts and Roman legions. And of the small dispersed remainder, countless others to the Cross, to crusaders and flagellants, inquisitors and Haidamuks and Cossacks. . . . In every generation they have stood against us to destroy us. . . . And in mine, they almost succeeded. I read aloud from memory the roster of the German and Austrian killing places. Mauthausen, a very Austrian-*gemüt-lich* camp on the blue Danube, not far from Wr. Neustadt, where the monthly death rate of Jews was nearly one hundred percent . . .

Almost. But never quite. Not even this century, not even here. Look —and I am nearly shouting now—look, look at us sitting at the wall. We are here. We were a community here before we were expelled six hundred years ago and our burial ground plowed up and the stones immured. We returned. Sixty years ago we once more fled for our lives. Now we are here again. See us. We are still here. We are old men and women of a very old people. We have been around for thousands of years and we shall continue to be around, a scourge to darkness, crying "Light!" Look well at my son and grandson. A century from now their children's children will chant the prayers on Friday night, as we shall now, as did the Oberrabbiner a few blocks down the street, and my mother's father, the *Kaiserlich-Königlicher Hofmaler,* in his flat a stone's throw from the royal residence of the Hapsburgs, and his father the rabbi in St. Pölten, and the ones before him in the Jewish alleyways of small towns in Niederösterreich and the border lands of Hungary and Slovakia. This is not only pride, I say, looking toward the curious passersby at the police barriers. It is my history.

I step aside. Yair takes my place in the center of the strip between the wall and the rows of chairs. Wrapped nearly from head to toe in my woolen *tallith,* much too large for him, he faces the stones, his back to the people, a small, erect figure enclosed from distraction in his assignment. In a clear voice he chants the opening Psalms of the Sabbath and the hymn of welcome to the Queen that is sung in every place Jews come together for prayer, the *Lechoh dodi*—"Come, my friend, to meet the Bride, the Sabbath, the Queen . . ." The words were written in the mid-sixteenth century by Shlomo Halevi Alkabetz, in Safed, a mountain town in the north of Israel. A circle of mystics had made their home there. On Friday afternoons they would walk down the slopes toward the mist rising at dusk from the Sea of Galilee and sing in the Sabbath. But the going out to greet the Sabbath goes back, much further, to the time of the Talmud. Rabbi Yannai would robe himself in festive garments and walk into the twilight calling, "Come, O Bride, Come, O Bride" and Rabbi Chaninah sang to his students, "Come, and we will go to meet the Bride, the Queen!" Tonight Yair is saluting her in Wr. Neustadt. There are many melodies to which the *Lechoh dodi* is sung. He chooses one common in the synagogues of modern Israel.

Our people join in. They know the tune, of course. Many of them have slipped away from tradition, but tonight . . . tonight the erosion of years, the compliances with modernity and secularism, are gone and we all are once more Jews of the Seven Communities on the eve of the sanctified day.

Hillie takes the *tallith* from Yair and leads *Aravith,* the statutory prayer cycle of night. When the service is over, we who have returned remain sitting for several long minutes. It is very still, as sometimes it is when something big and mystifying has happened with people. Some are weeping. Then a woman from a Socialist, *Shomer Hatzair* kibbutz in the Jordan Valley breaks the silence. "I am not a believer," she says to me, "but I know your father's spirit hovered over the wall tonight. Yes. There were four generations of you making *Schabbes* (the old Ashkenazi pronunciation) with us."

We return to the hotel. "*Shabbath shalom, Shabbath shalom,*" we wish each other and our Austrian guests. The ballroom downstairs is ours for the night. It is crowded. More than two hundred people. The Ichthys congregation and other friends are sharing the rich Sabbath repast provided by the caterer. The tables are decked with white cloths. There are spring flowers and bottles of sweet wine from Israel on each table. We stand for the *kiddush* and the breaking of the bread; Hillie has brought traditional *challah* twist loaves from a bakery in Jerusalem. The meal is served.

It is customary to sing verses of celebration, of the Sabbath's gifts and beauty, between the courses of the meal. Many of the poems are very old, the language Aramaic or ornate liturgical Hebrew, the first letters of the lines forming acrostics of the medieval poets' names. Scores of tunes have accrued for each poem among the scattered communities of the Diaspora, the tunes—the *niggunim*—cherished features of a community's distinctive order of service. The tunes have a holiness. In Jewish mysticism, all music is held to be sacred, of the spirit. *Hasidic* rebbes

roamed the countryside to gather up the strains of a Ukrainian shepherd's pipe, a weary Polish plower's air, and bring them back to the
shtetl, sounds of yearning or rejoicing. Some of the Sabbath table songs
are such tunes, melodies without words.

Four-fifths of all *hasidim* in the world perished in the Holocaust, I
suddenly recall.

A song begins, at first hesitatingly, at one of the tables. It is led by
the four Breuer girls. They are my age, they are all married, but they are
still the Breuer girls. Four of them. That is something of a wonder, all
the children of one family, who could not get out until very late, at the
end of 1939 or in the early 1940s, when only a very few still made it, and
they did. They had gone down the Danube on some sort of a craft. It
foundered, they fell into Italian hands in Yugoslav territory, and they
lived through the war protected in Italian army detention. They came
to Palestine, they have remained religious, they know the Sabbath
songs well and they can sing. The song takes on confidence and volume. Within minutes we are all in it. It is 9 o'clock.

Now, just before midnight, the tables have been pushed aside. We
are dancing between them, around them. In a cleared space in the middle of the room David Walter Riegler and I are doing a folk dance from
the *shtetl*, left hand high, waving to the beat, the right grasping a corner of a handkerchief that pairs the dancers, legs kicking out wildly,
creaking. One of the Roman priests leaps in, making it a trio. We belt
out at the top of our voices the stanza of a one-line song, *"David, melech
yisrael, chai, chai, v'kayom"*—David King of Israel, lives, he lives, he is—
the song to which the men and women of my synagogue in Jerusalem
dance through the streets on the autumn festival of Simchath Torah,
down to the Old City and the Western Wall, our Torah scrolls held high
beneath the canopy of a blue-striped *tallith*, one of my grandchildren on
my shoulders. Now we shift to Shlomo Carlebach's *niggun*, *"Am yisrael
chai, am yisrael chai . . . od avinu chai"*—the people of Israel lives, our father in heaven still lives. Hand on shoulder, hand on shoulder, sway-
ing lines of dancers are weaving through the room. Jackets and ties
have been discarded. We have exhausted the Sabbath table melodies we
know, Ashkenazi, Ladino, North African, Yemenite, and the melodies of
the *Hasidim* of Mozizh, Belz, Lubavich, Ger, Slonim. . . . We turn to the
more recent ones of the religious youth movements of Israel, and then
to the songs of the *chalutzim*, the young pioneers of the early *aliyoth* who

wrested milk and honey once more from the valleys of Yezreel, Beit Shean, the Hula, from swamp and parched hillside. *Ha'mamtirah*—the Sprinkler—and we form a circle and dance the drumming *horah* of the cascading drops of water sprayed by the hard-come-by tool that made the soil pliant to plow and spade. What precisely we sing and dance this night matters little. We have lost ourselves in rhythm, in a continuum, shed our reserve, shed our guard, not needed, for we are a strong people, the sturdiness of thirty-five hundred years of defying the probabilities.

People are looking in at the windows. The waiters are clustered at the kitchen door, staring. They have relinquished any attempt at wading in to clear the tables and serve coffee. One, an elderly man, says to me, *"Wissens, Herr Doktor, so was hat sich in Wiener Neustadt in a Hotel noch nie gegeben, aa nicht vor '38!,"* and then, puzzled, *"Das is aber a Wunder, a Geheimniss!"*—You know, Doctor, nothing like this ever happened in a Wr. Neustadt hotel, not even before '38; it's a wonder, a secret! A secret. The word brings an association, the last lines of Mark Twain's 1899 essay on the Jews:

> He has made a marvelous fight in the world, in all the ages; and he has done it with his hands tied behind him. . . . The Egyptian, the Babylonian, and the Persian rose, filled the planet with sound and splendor, then faded to dream-stuff and passed away; the Greeks and the Romans followed, and made a vast noise, and they are gone; other people have sprung up and held their torch high for a time, but it burned out, and they sit in twilight now, or have vanished. The Jew saw them all, beat them all, and is now what he always was, exhibiting no decadence, no infirmities of age, no weakening of his parts, no slowing of his energies. . . . All things are mortal but the Jew: all forces pass, but he remains. What is the secret of his immortality?

I look about me. Cohorts of fearsome warriors? Race of Titans? I see forty old, arthritic men and women hopping and shouting, dry bones of the host of Israel. But then, they really are not dry . . .

So many other associations.

David the shepherd, King of Israel, dancing with the common folk, among the handmaids of his servants, leaping before the Lord with all his might, the skirts of his linen tunic flying, as they brought the

Ark from the house of Oved-Edom to Jerusalem, and Michal the noble daughter of Saul came out to sneer at him in his abandonment. Michal had no child to the day of her death; David is forever *Melech Yisrael.*

The elders of the Jewish communities of White Russia forced by mocking troops, Germans and Austrians, to a *danse macabre* on broken glass, earlocks sliced off, beards singed, before being led off to the shooting pits in the forest.

We dance in abandonment at the Corvinus tonight. No, the bones have not withered.

We turn in in the early hours of morning.

SATURDAY

Stunned by These Days

Another get-together with students this morning, this time at the classical Gymnasium—the *Bundesgymnasium*—where my father taught religion and where I began the first year of high school that came to an abrupt end with the Anschluss. I am drained and I badly wanted this day without schedule. The Eiwens' program for Saturday reads, *"Der ganze Tag ist frei"*—the day is free. But Johannes Vrbecky is on the faculty, and I committed myself when I arrived at the airport in Vienna to this second engagement with young people, another "witnessing to a time."

The *Direktor* receives us in his office. There is a small crucifix on the wall above his desk. The Catholic disposition is not surprising, although this is not a parochial institution. It is, rather, emblematic of the primary standing of the Roman Church in this country. When I was a pupil there were parallel classes in the grades, one for the Catholic children, one for Lutherans and Jews.

I am received warmly over coffee and *Kuchen.* The professors who join us make no attempt to glide over the dark past of which I am to make personal attestation. To my question about the students' political inclinations, I am told that neo-Nazi attitudes are not to be found here in the Gymnasium, but yes, they are not unknown in the city's trade schools. The conversation is frank, the teachers in the room clearly are intent on having their charges hear at first hand from a would-be alumnus accounts that most of their elders prefer forgotten, but I miss the unsparing dedication of Marianne Neuber.

We walk to the assembly hall down a long corridor. Pictures of former mentors line the passage. I recognize several from my truncated year. One was given to anti-Semitic comments from the cathedra. The photograph of my father which Johannes had requested from me is to join the row.

Again, about two hundred earnest teenagers. My talk, the questions and discussions afterward, are a replica of the confrontation a few days ago at the *Realgymnasium.*

Helmuth Eiwen was right: There is a chance here with this generation, there is a willingness to know, there is a responsiveness. But how much of a chance? One such occasion, a few . . . how much of a dent can they make against this society's thrust to forget, to gloss over, to deny? "It is not incumbent on you to complete the task, neither are you free to desist from it," the *Mishnah* presses. True. Put my shoulder to the salvage of the children of the inflictors. Important. Perhaps essential. I shall do the best I can, now that I have somehow been pressed to it, but the task, here, in *eretz hadamim,* this bloody land, is not one I would have elected. My guts rebel at it. Yet . . . my heart and mind have been touched by many of the people I have come to know this week. Conflicting organic signals. I am, truly, honestly, bone weary.

Lunch at Toni Macheiner's, Johannes Vrbecky's genial parishioner. It is a special family occasion, the thirtieth wedding anniversary of the Macheiners. Only Johannes and I have been invited. Toni knows some of the Jewish dietary rules from his trip to Israel, and Johannes had apparently amplified earlier in the week. There are fresh-caught trout baked in butter. And there is, again, one of those added touches of sweetness that so unexpectedly have been extended to me and the others on this return; Toni has gone beyond my own *kashruth* scruples. He bought a new cooking pan so that I would enjoy the hospitality without second thought, knowing that even the utensils met *halachic* standards; he purchased the pan at the hardware store on Hauptplatz 11, where sixty years ago the rabbi's wife, my mother, had gone for her kitchen ware.

We are in the garden, admiring the flowers and the hedges in early blossom. We talk of fish and fishing, of the game up in the distant mountains that are sharply etched against the midday sky, of hikes with backpacks to remote places. I tell of small adventures in the empty stretches of the Negev, in Savuti and the Okavango Delta, the Engadine highlands, the canyons of Amazonia, the arctic tundra of Canada's Northwest Territory. And it occurs to me that I am comfortable.

I reflect: The Catholics who have held out their hand to me here, and in Jerusalem when I met with Johannes's church group, speak very little of guilt and contrition. Not Johannes, not the brothers at the Neukloster. None of them, really, as my mind scans the roster. Not even Marianne, who is so shaken by what she knows of the past, who could not stop the tears when, half a year later, she was in Washington and we stood before the ghastly exhibits of cattle cars and starved skeletons at the Holocaust museum. Marianne is a patriotic Austrian, she loves the country of her birth and life. So do Johannes and Toni. Nonetheless they know. They don't play games with the record, and they reach out, but they are unlike the Eiwens and their congregation whose deep religiosity centers on enunciative remorse. In a way, I find myself more at ease with the unspoken. Perhaps because then one is not steadily drawn back to the unthinkable, there is a wider space, a less burdened Now, in which to meet the outstretched hand.

I compliment our host on the excellent Wachauer we are drinking. It came from a vineyard and winery Toni owns with some friends. It is the next to last bottle of an outstanding vintage, he explains. When I leave, it is with the gift of the last bottle. Toni insists I take it home.

In January 1996 I have a letter from him. That Christmas was the first when the crèche beneath the tree was not one of theirs; it was, rather, the one of olive wood I had bought them from an Arab carver in Bethlehem. As Pater Johannes proclaimed the glad tidings at Midnight Mass in the Neukloster, Toni's thoughts were not only with the place in the Holy Land where it happened, but "also with you Dr. Weiss in Jerusalem." And he continues, *"Lieber David, es ist jetzt schon wieder fast ein Jahr her, dass es mir vergönnt war, einen Menschen kennenzulernen, welcher durch seine konziliante Haltung für mich das Judentum einer völlig neuen Betrachtungsweise zugeführt hat und dafür möchte ich mich herzlich bedanken"*—nearly a year has passed since it was granted me to meet a person who by his conciliatory attitude has led me to a wholly new perspective of Jewry, for which my warm thanks.

The dictionary renders the word "conciliate" as "to overcome distrust or hostility; placate; win over; reconcile."

Johannes has told me, in one of his many calls the months after the week, what Toni had confided in him: His brief relationship with David Weiss was of some consequence. Toni had held, without much thought, to the plebeian anti-Semitic stereotypes that in Austria, as in many European countries, seep through the generations, a thing of the blood. One doesn't have to know a Jew to be an anti-Semite, Gregor von Rezzori maintained. I didn't seem to fit a stereotype.

Evening. The last scheduled event of the *Woche*, a parting dinner at the hotel. The Ichthys congregation is there, and Johannes Vrbecky, and some of the others with whom we met. The children of our hosts sing and dance for us a last time. Farewell speeches by Helmuth and Uli and Johannes. This shall be the first of such comings together, the Eiwens promise; their determination is unmistakable. They bless us in the name of the God of Abraham, Isaac, and Jacob who consoles and protects his people Israel.

Pater Johannes is brief and straightforward. He thanks the Eiwens and their community for having brought about this week. The Church is too ponderous to have done that. Unless it expunges from its collective oeuvre the nuances of hostility to the Jews it cannot stand clean before God; he states that as a simple matter of fact.

Throughout the talks there runs an outpouring of affection that is almost staggering, for all that it has been expressed so often this week by word and gesture.

When we compare notes later, all of us who have returned, even those who were the most doubting and reserved, admit that we are stunned by these days. We are caught up in a connectedness for which we were not prepared and which we did not seek. When we leave it is with the feeling of something newly discovered and moving in this place full of hateful memories.

SUNDAY

At Sauerbrunn the Wild Strawberries Are Gone

Hillie and Yair are taken by one of the Ichthys couples to the airport for the flight home. I had promised Johannes to stay on until tomorrow and spend this day with him. No formalities, only a circuit of calls on friends who must get to know me.

The first stop is in Sauerbrunn. The blue and white stucco villa that was our summer home no longer stands. The rutted path that led to

Wiesen is now a paved country road, and the sunny meadow sloping down from the edge of the forest on which my sister and I were allowed to run free and pick sweet wild strawberries—well in sight of the house—is densely settled by other people's cottages. I am not even sure just where on the Wiesenweg our villa and garden had been.

Sacher Torte, Linzer Torte, Strudel, and Gugelhupf, Kaffee mit Schlag are set out at each stop. One may decline the first offer and the second, but not a third. I am on good behavior and struggle to cope. Johannes presents me as his dear friend. Welcome, we are happy you have come, they all greet me. Some make it more difficult. We are so glad you have come home, *ja natürlich* it was hard for you, we understand, but you are back in the *Heimat, das Mutterland bleibt doch immer*— the motherland always remains—once an Austrian always an Austrian. No, I think, most of them don't understand. An old lady launches into the prevailing catechism: We had no idea where the Jewish neighbors had gone, they simply weren't there one day, no one knew what had become of them, no one could guess the bad things of which we heard only after the war, that was the work of the Nazis, the S.S. and the Gestapo, all Austrians were afraid of them. . . . She is interrupted abruptly by a daughter-in-law, a physician. Nonsense, she exclaims, we knew very well, there are no excuses, we can only be ashamed. Others stay meticulously away from the past and talk about the weather and the countryside. One gentleman, a young engineer, would have me persuaded that Jörg Haider, the leader of the far-right party that has been gaining strength at the polls, is unjustly besmirched as a neo-Nazi by the liberals and socialists. The former Waffen-S.S. officers prominent in the party's upper echelons . . . one must acknowledge, he insists, that the S.S. combat divisions were honorable soldiers, innocent of the excesses committed by . . . someone else. That, of course, is a lie, naked and convenient. The Waffen-S.S. participated in the murder of Jews and of civilians in occupied lands and of prisoners of war with not much greater scruple than did the selectively appointed killing units. The engineer pursues my enlightenment of Mr. Haider's reasonable, patriotic character. The party's agitation against foreign workers, that must be understood against the background of intolerable social and economic problems posed by the influx of so vastly alien an element. And may I not press you to have another bite of the excellent *Kuchen*? He is really quite charming, intelligent and urbane. I wonder: How familiar it all rings, how easily the old, deadly roles of patriot and villain can come to life again in a new cast of players here on a balmy Sunday afternoon over dessert.

MONDAY

Last Breakfast at the Neukloster

After the meal, after I have recited the Hebrew grace, Pater Otto, the oldest of the Cistercians—he is in his eighties—rises for a word of farewell. What he says is really addressed to the other priests. I would say to you, he begins, that I believe we are indebted to our guest. I believe we can learn from him what a religious life is truly like. We, we strive in quietude to answer to our obligations as the day brings them before us. We serve in hallowed precincts. We walk our cloisters, we recite our rosary, we contemplate. But he—Pater Otto points to me and his low voice rises—he *lives* his faith. He is of this world and he lives his belief. See, the *Käppchen*—the little cap—on his head, it is always on him. He lives his faith when he walks and when he is at table and when he rests on his Sabbath. That is a living faith. He can teach us. I salute him.

Pater Otto knows nothing of my waywardness, my many lapses from the covenant. It hits me hard: He, this Cistercian priest of Jesus of Nazareth, has very quietly, without knowing it, called me to account. Shame floods through me. As it had when a devout admired master in *yeshivah* praised me for something I knew to have been little more than show. These are things held hidden in the heart. It is of them, the Talmud declares, that Scripture speaks when it bids to fear the Lord our God. The priest knows me little. I am caught short of the belief he has placed in me. Is that not a kind of betrayal? Do I not owe him a hard searching of the heart? A person who has taught one a single *halachah*, one paradigm of behavior, is regarded as one's rebbe, one's teacher. That, too, is an epigram of the Talmud.

And sixty years ago a Jewish boy would bypass this house of enmity where they worshipped the god whose blood they put on our heads.

Johannes drives me to the airport. We stop for coffee in Baden, where my mother's father received the Hapsburg crown prince on a Sabbath afternoon sitting at table for the mystic Third Meal of the day of rest, and where my sister was born.

I take a flight to New York, to a workshop on immunology. Then I will return home, to Israel.

Chapter 15

WHAT THE PASTOR OF ICHTHYS HAS CAUGHT IN HIS NET

AFTERWARD, 1995 . . .

"Sorry, but I can't stay late tonight," my wife explains to her co-workers at the Social Services offices in Jerusalem, "I have to get home to make dinner for my priest."

When Johannes comes to Israel he stays with us. We take trips together to the remnants of the ancient Phoenician and Roman cities on the coast, to Crusader castles, the nature preserves in the Hula and the headwaters of the Jordan at Tel Dan. The friendship between us has broadened and deepened, we call each other often, report our daily lives, as if we were relatives who wish to preserve family ties from loosening.

I meet with the groups of Catholic tourists and pilgrims Johannes periodically brings to the country. There are sessions of talk at the Kings Hotel down the block from where we live, questions-and-answers about Jews and Judaism, the situation in Israel. The visitors are concerned about the relations between Jews and Arabs, Israelis and Palestinians. I try to be objective. I am also passionately an advocate of our cause. That is not always an easy synthesis. European media do not go out of their way to present a balanced picture of the Jewish State; I have little trouble pinpointing distortions, setting the record straight. At the same time, my wife and I are active in the process toward the elusive goal of peace, and we have found ourselves squarely with the opposition to the government that came into power in the spring of 1996. There have been policies and actions that I cannot defend among ourselves, and I cannot stretch advocacy to a blind apologetic, not even when I speak to outsiders.

The groups who travel with Johannes are people of good will; yet, the cursed past is always there, intruder into the present. They cannot help referring, again and again, to what was, they must show regret and sympathy, they speak of the unspeakable as a walker navigates his way on early winter ice. Yes, they are, most of them, decent, ordinary men and women, but ordinary men did the unspeakably indecent. Those who now sit with me in the lobby of the Kings are embarrassed for what was done and don't know what to do about it. They are not like the extraordinary Ichthys people or like Johannes or Marianne Neuber.

An elderly man tries to convince me that not all Austrians were guilty. Only one-third, he maintains, were actively involved, a third indifferent, a third disliked what they saw but dared not interfere. Only a third and another third, and all I can think is, My God, that is a grace? But he truly means well, he is setting out to put a better face on ugliness, he is an Austrian and he cannot condemn in their entirety the people to which he was born. I understand that. He is not aware that the statistics on which he leans are themselves a condemnation. He makes no facile equations between the Six Million and the deprivations his countrymen suffered in war and defeat. I believe he is a good man and knows not what his words say.

One Friday night, several of Johannes's travelers join him for dinner with us. They look at the photographs of my family that hang framed in my study. One is of my father, the dashing cavalry captain on the Russian front in 1916, his medals affixed to the picture's corners. In another he is surrounded by men of his battalion. They are posing at the entrance of an improvised barrack. That photograph was snapped minutes before the hut was hit by a shell. Another photo is of my *Kaiserlich-Königlicher Hofmaler* grandfather, standing at an easel with the still unfinished portrait of a distinguished personage of the Emperor's court. The visitors are enthusiastic. Austrians cherish great nostalgia for the bygone days of Franz Joseph's harmlessly decrepit Empire. My study is filled floor to ceiling with Jewish tomes, the *mezuzoth* on doors are large, the appurtenances of a parochial identity visible throughout the house; there are also Japanese woodcuts and African artifacts and Inuit soapstone carvings; but all the confusing foreignness recedes before the symbols of membership in the club of old Hapsburg Österreich. The guests eagerly tell me of their fathers' and grandfathers' uniforms and insignia, they were so similar. We are a brotherhood, old Austrian stock. At dinner one of them reminisces about his own service, in World War II. He was in the *Luftwaffe*, shot down near Stalingrad, survived Russian imprisonment. Again the jarring. This is my Sabbath table in Jerusalem. What are these people doing here? What am I?

There is a steady flow of mail from Wr. Neustadt and the neighboring towns. Good wishes for the High Holydays, for Passover, greetings from summer vacations, announcements of events in families we had come to know that week.

Some of the letters are more than affirmations of regard.

Werner Sulzgruber and Gerhard Michram are preparing dissertations on Jewish communities that flourished in Niederösterreich before the Nazis put them out. Robert Sommer writes from Vienna that he is working on a book to be called *Jewish Sauerbrunn*. The spa was a popular resort for Jewish vacationers and "on the occasion of forthcoming anniversary celebrations this long repressed—*verdrängte und tabusierte*—aspect of Sauerbrunn's history should thoroughly be brought to light." Could I provide information for their work? the writers ask.

Carola Tengler writes from Pitten with a different request. The Week has "driven her to learn much more about the *Greueltaten*—the atrocities—that were inflicted on the Jewish people. . . . That knowledge has led me to a profound sense of penitence. . . . My plea for forgiveness from the merciful Lord is now no longer for the deeds and silence of my German and Austrian countrymen, it is for deeds of my own family. I am no longer interested just to assign guilt; I want to take up the search for survivors so that I can reach my hand to them. Can you help me in my search?" She gives me the names of two Jews, a man and a woman who lived in Gross-Gerau, the town in Germany where Carola was born, and her own maiden name. The man left for Palestine in 1937; she believes he is on the faculty of Hebrew University. She is right. I make inquiries and find him. Carola establishes contact. The woman was arrested by the police in June of 1933 and Carola knows nothing further of her. Of her I can discover no trace.

Another such request arrives by FAX from Australia. Franz Selch has seen a brief article on the Week that appeared in *The Jerusalem Report*. I quote Mr. Selch's letter pro verbatim:

> The article has touched my wife and I very deeply since I was born not 10 KM from Wiener Neustadt, in Schwarzau am Steinfeld. As far as I know there was only one Jewish family in Schwarzau who had owned the local Grocery Store. My family was befriended with them, but they vanished suddenly about the time of the Anschluss and nothing more was heard of them. I am not certain about the spelling of their name, but it was either Eibert or Öbert; maybe you know of their fate or whereabouts—my mother would be interested to know since our family also suffered persecution on account of their friendship with the Jewish family. We would like to get in touch with that Austrian pastor, Helmut Eiwen, because my wife and I have been involved in the fight against antisemitism in the Australian Churches for many years. Regrettably there is insufficient information in the article for us to make contact, so we hope that you would kindly assist us.

The letter is signed by him over Hebrew that spells "Shalom." I send Helmuth's address, but I cannot help with the search for the grocer and his family. No trace.

Correspondence with Herwig Strobl, who so beautifully played Klezmer music for us that evening in the Sparkassensaal. This is the last letter I have from him; I translate it in full:

> Since I broke free of the unholy history of my family my life has changed. Much new has opened for me, for which I am grateful. Pain in the beginning, but there has grown in me much strength and love for human beings. I am so glad that we exchange these lines. I think that you know much of sadness and of what is incomprehensible, I only a little of that. I feel linked with you. . . . Yes, certainly, I have stood in the chapel at Hadassah—the Chagall—And I hardly dare hope that one day my wish may come true to play our music (yes: our music) in Israel. Shalom.

Helmuth and Uli were right. It is not for nothing that I returned.

Beatrix Bastl, the archivist of Wr. Neustadt, reminds me of a promise to let her see whatever documents and memorabilia I have kept, in long unopened drawers, that pertain to the Oberrabbiner, the community, the *Tempel*.

Marianne Neuber. We communicate often. The first student exchange has taken place. A high school class from Bat Yam, south of Tel Aviv, flew to Vienna, accompanied by their principal and a teacher. The teacher was Naomi Beinhacker, now Shifrin; her brother Xendi was my friend until our families had to flee their different ways. Marianne organized their stay in Wr. Neustadt singlehandedly, up against the disinclination of many of her associates at the *Realgymnasium*. The visit was a great success. The parents of Marianne's pupils housed the Israeli teenagers. Affections flowered between young hosts and guests. The Austrians are now planning a reciprocal visit to their new friends in Bat Yam. I shall pitch in to smooth arrangements, and I am in touch with an Arab school near Jerusalem to make the experience tripartite.

And the Eiwens of Ichthys . . . I would like to write "Helmuth and Uli von Ichthys," the "von" as preceding the patronymic of nobility, for they are that.

They persist in scouring the world for Wr. Neustadt Jews. They are finding many more than I knew to be still living, and the children of others who died. The discoveries are made known to us by word and in newsletters that every so often arrive at our doors, the masthead depicting a *menorah* and, in Hebrew letters in bold type, the prophet's consolation, "Comfort ye, comfort ye, my people." Memory's hold on the disappeared community of my childhood has grown stronger. Names and faces that almost faded have taken shape. That is important to me, strangely perhaps. I have always seen myself as standing solidly in the moment of the Now, poised for the moments ahead. But then, the sentience of present and future is in so many ways aligned with past experience and sensibility; a past wiped out leaves one with a dubious compass. The importance is not, after all, so strange. I understand myself better this day as I can unravel strands that lead back to days long before.

The findings of the Eiwens are mine as well.

Fred Landau now lives in Wales. I had no recollection of him, we were not close. Now we write and I remember. Hours playing in the garden of his Aunt Elfi. One afternoon she had whispered to my mother of a neighbor's decline. The illness was not to be mentioned by name.

Later I wanted to know why *Krebs*—the crab, cancer—was a shameful thing, was it a lewdness? No, my mother said, it is a scourge, and one day it will be understood and cured. Elfi's uncle was Chief Rabbi of South Africa. I was fascinated by the stamps on a letter from Johannesburg lying on her coffee table. And . . . now I remember . . . when the uncle retired there was talk of my father's accepting the post, and of his decision not to; he was at home with his congregation on the Baumkirchnerring, and with Wr. Neustadt.

Frank Goldner, a nuclear engineer who lives in Baltimore and is back and forth to Chernobyl to advise on the disaster's containment. Frank has reminded me of a day in the early 1940s when my father married his parents, both also refugees, in his study on Seventh Street on the Lower East Side. I held one of the rods of the royal blue canopy. Worn thin and frayed, the cloth now decorates one of the sidings of our Jerusalem *Sukkah*.

Gertie Popper. I knew nothing of her for nearly sixty years. Then Helmuth gave me a number in Wisconsin and when I heard her voice there swam before my eyes the grave face of Advokat Dr. Popper, her father, and even more clearly the red hair of the girl, and it came to me that I have always had a weak spot for crimson shocks of disorder framing a woman's freckled face, and that the swarms of carmine bee-eaters that ride the back of Kori bustards as they lumber through high grass on Botswana prairies, scaring up clouds of insects, evoke images of a bevy of girls fluttering about.

Helmuth and Uli have cast a wide net. When they travel, on the Continent, in Great Britain, in Israel, and the States, they stay with families from our town. Acquaintance amplifies. Since *Die Woche* in 1995 three other Weeks of Return have taken place. As I write, these last days of 1997, another is in the planning. People come who could not earlier, some have been guests more than once. But we are aging fast and our numbers are dwindling—there are, for all the Eiwens' searching, only so many of us left—and Helmuth and Uli, tireless, are directing the effort at the second generation of survivors.

Carola Tengler has fashioned a ceramic tablet commemorating the Friday night when Hillie and Yair prayed in the Sabbath at the old wall. The tablet is mounted next to the row of medieval Jewish gravestones.

The menorah we brought for Ichthys is making a circuit of Free Churches in America. The silver symbol of the ancient Temple and of the Jewish commonwealth that was and is again stands to alert Christian memory and Christian conscience.

The evening after the first day of the Passover this year, Helmuth called. He was unusually animated. Uli and he and a dozen of the Ichthys people made the Seder, a real Seder, for Herta Gerstl. I had been mistaken. There *is* one Jew left in the counties, Herta. She is very old and frail and confined to a flat in Neunkirchen. She could not travel to the community in Vienna. So the Eiwens went to her, with matzah, the unleavened bread of affliction, and bitter herbs, with baked egg and roasted shankbone for the Seder plate. They read for her the order of the story of the Exodus from the *haggadah.* The Cup of Elijah, who walks unknown forever among the Jewish people and tarries a moment that night at each Jewish home when the songs of redemption are sung, they filled with wine from the Judean hills so that the wanderer could take his unseen sip, even there.

What the pastor of Ichthys and his wife have caught up in their net are the last stragglers of a lost company. Enmeshed, like cells in a reticulum, the Jews of Wr. Neustadt are once more adherent in a commonality, stretched very thin, very tenuous, but, yes, a commonality, a *kehillah.*

Chapter 16

WHEN ONE STANDS
FACE TO FACE

DECEMBER 1997, JERUSALEM

I should like to weave these themes of return into a fresh motif, a new, integrated perception, like the coda of a symphonic movement. But that is not easy.

When I read another Holocaust account, see another exhibition of brutal death, there wells up in me, as it always has, the uncomprehending, nauseated revulsion and the reflex to strike out blindly at the nations who so nearly extinguished mine.

But I can no longer reach for the imaginary button that would send them all, all that is German and Austrian, to the bottom of the sea.

I am a son of the covenant. That has been held before my eyes. My father Abraham fought unsparingly with the Lord Judge of all the earth for the lives of Sodom and Gomorrah . . . perhaps fifty righteous souls there . . . if but forty, twenty, only ten . . .

I have come to know more than that in my town.

That is not, intellectually, a revelation. That there were men and women who did not condone the barbarity, who risked life in the opposing, that is not new. The trees lining the Avenue of the Righteous Among the Nations at Yad Vashem bear witness to them. But information is not always knowing.

The week of my return and what went before and came thereafter brought a knowing that is not abstract, not arithmetic. I met, head-on, with faces.

The early imprints of place and language came to the fore in me that week. Some mistook the reawakened familiarity for something more, for a fresh grafting to severed roots. There has been no such reconciliation, no restoring of an Austrian identity. My self-definition has not expanded.

What has expanded is a commitment to the salience of the individual. For me that can no longer be a platitude, drawn upon occasion from a repertoire of condescending rhetoric. The return was a confrontation, flesh and blood, with the singularity of which men and women —ordinary men and women—are capable. It was for me a palpable confirmation of belief in a human future, in the potential of the self even in wastelands.

David W. Weiss,

born to an old and distinguished Jewish family in Austria,
fled as a child with his parents and sister from Nazi persecution, reaching the United States in 1939. He earned a Ph.D. in
microbiology at Rutgers University and a D.Phil. in medicine
from Oxford University. Formerly professor of bacteriology
and immunology at the University of California at Berkeley,
in 1966 he immigrated to Israel, where he founded and directed the Lautenberg Center for General and Tumor Immunology at Hebrew University in Jerusalem. In addition to numerous publications in biomedical science, Weiss is the author of
works on Jewish law and philosophy, including *The Wings of
the Dove: Jewish Values, Science, and Halachah.*

28
X DAYS

GAYLORD M2